VIETNAM and ARMAGEDDON

PEACE, WAR AND THE CHRISTIAN CONSCIENCE

VIETNAM and ARMAGEDDON

PEACE, WAR AND THE CHRISTIAN CONSCIENCE

by Robert F. Drinan, S.J.

SHEED AND WARD • NEW YORK

© Sheed and Ward, Inc., 1970
Library of Congress Catalog Card Number: 71-101550
Standard Book Number: 8362-0484-0
Manufactured in the United States of America

IMPRIMI POTEST
William G. Guindon, S.J.
Provincial, New England Province
Society of Jesus

IMPRIMATUR
✠Richard Cardinal Cushing
Archbishop of Boston
February 2, 1970

Contents

VIETNAM and ARMAGEDDON

PEACE, WAR AND THE CHRISTIAN CONSCIENCE

Foreword

THE WRITING of this book became necessary for me during a week spent in South Vietnam with a group of Americans sent by the Fellowship of Reconciliation to investigate the state of religious and political freedom in that tragic land. I discovered in Saigon that the Catholics of South Vietnam, because of their fear of communism, are solidly in favor of the war. Their attitude was similar to that of many if not most American Catholics who have favored a hard line against communism—even by the use of war, if necessary.

The appalling and agonizing tragedies so omnipresent in Vietnam caused me to realize with acute pain that neither the Holy See nor the American bishops have given any of us strong leadership or guidance on one of the most awful events of our age—a war which has taken the lives of over one million persons, which has caused the dislocation of ev-

1

ery fourth Vietnamese, and which has turned two million people into refugees.

Even the moral theologians have been mute about the most pressing moral and ethical question of our day: Can one country justifiably kill countless individuals and devastate a nation in order to prevent the domination of seventeen million South Vietnamese by a political group whose philosophical roots, according to the proponents of the war, are in materialism and Marxism?

The question pressed upon my mind in the tropical heat of Saigon. The question, of course, is of incalculable importance since other nations in the "Third World" will soon have their own revolutions followed by counterinsurgencies. Should America or SEATO or any alliance of nations make commitments to use their collective and highly sophisticated military strength to keep insurgent nations out of the Communist bloc? Will such commitments inevitably lead to a form of genocide in that two highly industrialized nations will be devastating an underdeveloped country in order to try to prove the superiority of their own technocracy and power of endurance? The question has indescribable importance for that half of the human race who lives in Asia.

There are several possible reasons to explain the almost total silence of the hierarchies of America and South Vietnam about the tragic war in which their nations are engaged. In each country Catholics are in a minority—1.8 million out of 17 million in South Vietnam, and 46 million out of 200 million in the United States. The war, moreover, is such a tangled web of contradictions involving international law and Cold War diplomacy that Catholic bishops perhaps should not be expected to enunciate any moral norms by which the justness of the war could be resolved. Thirdly, one could argue that Catholic doctrine about war cannot be expected to be more specific than Pope John put it in *Pacem in Terris* (for excerpts of this encyclical, see Appendix B), or than it was stated in the January 1968 statement of the thirteen bishops of South Vietnam or in the November 1968 message of the American bishops.

The relative silence of Catholics about the morality of the Vietnam war is made more difficult to understand by the almost unanimous sentiment among Protestant theologians that the Vietnam war is morally indefensible. Professor Paul Ramsey of Princeton Theological Seminary is almost the only major theologian among nonevangelical American Protestants to find any moral justification for the American position in Vietnam. In his book, *The Just War: Force and Political Responsibility,* * Dr. Ramsey argues persuasively that his fellow Protestant theologians have conducted their war against the Vietnam war on the basis of a pragmatic quasi-pacifism and not on moral or theological principles common to Protestant tradition. While disclaiming any obsession against communism, Dr. Ramsey points out that Protestant scholars in America who are "doves" with regard to the war in Vietnam have not justified their position in view of their overwhelming support of America's position in World War II and their silence with respect to the U.S. position in the Korean conflict. Professor Ramsey, in short, challenges Protestant opposition as being excessively humanitarian and crypto-pacifist without knowing or admitting it. We shall give more detailed attention to his position in later pages.

The opposition of Vietnamese Buddhists to the war also makes the Catholic position in South Vietnam more difficult to comprehend. I did not fully appreciate the profound, although not universally held, opposition of Buddhists to the war fought by the South Vietnam government until I talked to many Buddhist leaders in Paris and in Saigon. The Buddhist position was made dramatically clear to me when, to my astonishment, I came upon a group of 120 Buddhist monks in a Saigon prison. The prison officials had built a temple for

*New York, Charles Scribner's Sons, 1968.

these head-shaven, celibate monks clad in the saffron robes of their monastery. The monks, some of whom were imprisoned for resistance to the draft and others because they had advocated peace rather than war, were permitted to pray in groups at their pagoda at different times during the day and night. The presence of monks in prison for reasons of conscience made it clear that Buddhism stood for nonviolence and for a profound respect for the inviolability of human life.

It would be an oversimplification, however, to suggest that Buddhist history or theology would outlaw all wars. Buddhism has too many national forms to permit such a generalization. As Kenneth K.S. Ch'en of Princeton University makes clear in his book, *Buddhism, the Light of Asia,* * Buddhism has an amazing capacity to adapt and to "baptize" a variety of diverse and even contradictory doctrines and cultures from many eras. There is nonetheless a strong and enduring teaching of nonviolence within Buddhism. This teaching has always been present in Vietnamese Buddhism despite the fact that the Vietnamese people fought against their Chinese overlords for a thousand years and against their French masters for almost a hundred years. The nonviolence and the love of peace which are so essential to Buddhism did not prompt all Buddhist officials in Vietnam to discourage or to deter those Vietnamese, in the South as well as in the North, who were inclined to use force against the American presence in Vietnam—a presence which many of them deemed to be even more unjustified than the French colonial government.

Despite the abiding and tenacious adherence to peace and nonviolence on the part of Buddhists in Vietnam, the Catholics in South Vietnam have apparently not been influenced towards any modification of their almost unanimous position that the Viet Cong and communism could and should be deterred and destroyed by military means. Catholics in South Vietnam have in fact given vigorous support to every an-

*Woodbury, New York: Barron's Educational Series, Inc., 1968.

ticommunist government since the withdrawal of the French after Dien Bien Phu. Hardly a dozen priests out of some thirteen hundred in South Vietnam have ever participated in any notable way in any religiously inspired movement for peace in South Vietnam.

In view, therefore, of the conflicting teachings of Catholics, Protestants, and Buddhists on a war in which all of these groups have a profound interest, it will be worthwhile to have a thorough review and analysis of every argument of a moral nature which these groups have used either to justify or to condemn the Vietnam war.

It is indeed distressing and humiliating to note that the Catholic Church, despite the enormous vitality and the new openness brought to it by Vatican II, has said virtually nothing of great moral consequence about the Vietnam war. Perhaps the Church's almost total silence about one of the greatest moral problems of this era may at least prompt a complete reexamination of the relevance, if any, of the Church's traditional teaching on the reasons which can make a war just. The silence of the Church may be due to an unresolved but unacknowledged massive doubt among Catholics as to the continued applicability or relevance of the Church's teaching on war and peace. That teaching was formulated long before war became fraught with thermonuclear horrors. That teaching, moreover, although relatively well developed in that Augustinian-Thomistic tradition, cannot be said to have had any highly visible effects in the last three centuries since the development of nationalism and colonialism, with all the wars which these twin dominating forces of Western culture have brought to the world.

When one examines the seeming ineradicability of war in Western history, one is tempted to wonder whether Christianity, instead of decreasing the likelihood of war by its teaching of love, has in fact intensified the opportunity for wars by furnishing the occasion for "holy wars" and "crusades." Clearly America's foreign policy since World War II, which has centered on the containment of communism—with its application in the Vietnam war—derives in part from a "crusade" to stop the progress of atheistic and materialistic Marxism. It is not possible therefore simply to say that the Catholic Church's teaching on a just war was not operative in the Vietnam war. As difficult and distasteful as the task may be, we must explore the possibility that the United States was in effect following the Catholic theory of the just war in the Vietnam struggle. Although even the most vigorous "doves" among the Catholic journals in America—*Commonweal* and the *National Catholic Reporter*—have not suggested that the United States has "baptized" and applied or misapplied the Catholic theory of a just war, the evidence for such a possibility is more abundant than most of us like to admit.

In order to obtain as clear an understanding as possible of what Catholics, Protestants, and Buddhists tried to say about the Vietnam war, it will be helpful to review in turn (1) what Vatican II stated about war; (2) what the American Catholic bishops said about their country's land war in Southeast Asia; (3) what views the World Council of Churches and the U.S. National Council of Churches expressed on the war; and (4) what opinions Vietnamese Buddhists tried, with little success, to make known to the world.

1.

Vatican II and War

SIX PAGES, or about twenty-five hundred words, in the *Pastoral Constitution on the Church in the Modern World* contain virtually all that Vatican II said about war. (See Appendix C.) The contents of this document, ratified by Pope Paul and the bishops on December 7, 1965, were discussed and approved by the Council fathers after they and the whole world knew of the major escalation in Vietnam launched by the United States government in February 1965. Despite the centrality for everyone in the world of the question of the ethics of intervention by one nation into the war of a far weaker nation, Vatican II did not address itself directly to this problem. Nor is there any clear record that the material on war considered in the 1964 session of the Council received any important change or modification as a result of the situation in Vietnam, where the total number of American soldiers in December 1965 was approaching one hundred thousand.

One of the most hopeful aspects of the Vatican II statement on war is the suggestion that, once a truly international body with juridical powers has been created, war will no longer be necessary or possible. The Council does not quite say how this will occur. Indeed the Council may have slipped into that widespread, unrealistic overconfidence in the power of what is called "world law."

Aside from this velleity, it is uncertain whether Vatican II resolved any of the dilemmas and ambiguities about nuclear war and the theories of deterrence which plague the modern world.

The Council asserts rather uncritically: "As long as the danger of war remains and there is no competent and sufficiently powerful authority at the international level, governments cannot be denied the right to legitimate defense once every means of peaceful settlement has been exhausted." This sentence seems to clash with a subsequent holding in which the Council speaks of being "compelled" to undertake an evaluation of war with an "entirely new attitude." Indeed the question can be justifiably raised whether anything at all contained in Vatican II's statement on war adopts the "entirely new attitude" on international conflict mandated by the Council.

Vatican II reiterates, although in a cautious, negative, and almost uncertain way, the traditional theory that war is justified if the conditions of necessity and the limitation of means are fulfilled. The Council did not expressly refer to the requirement of proportionality, but there is no evidence that its omission means anything except that it was deemed to be self-evident.

Vatican II, however, sets forth two moral principles as absolutes. By so doing the Council may well have inserted into a conciliar document principles which could eventually lead to a condemnation of all modern war. The first of these principles is the forbidding as "most infamous" those actions

"designed for the methodical extermination of an entire people, nation, or ethnic minority." The second principle condemns as a "crime against God and man himself ... any act
of war aimed indiscriminately at the destruction of entire
cities or extensive areas along with their population." Such an
act "merits unequivocal and unhesitating condemnation."

It seems reasonably clear that the Council fathers intended
in these two condemnations to go beyond the traditional
concept of immunity for noncombatants from direct attack.
It seems similarly clear that Vatican II did *not* intend to
condemn outright all modern war. But the real question
avoided (deliberately or otherwise) comes to this: If genocide
and "the destruction of ... extensive areas along with their
population" is subject to "unequivocal ... condemnation,"
then how can the possession of intercontinental ballistic missiles, designed precisely to achieve such objectives, be
deemed a moral act?

The Council fathers made some attempt to answer this
question, but in the end left it unresolved. The Council states
that the

> defensive strength of any nation is considered to be depend-
> ent upon its capacity for immediate retaliation against an ad-
> versary. Hence this accumulation of arms, which increases
> each year, also serves, in a way heretofore unknown, as a
> deterrent to possible enemy attack.

The Council goes on to concede that "many regard this
state of affairs as the most effective way by which peace of
a sort can be maintained between nations at the present
time." No footnote tells us about the qualifications of the
"many" who feel that "coexistence in terror" (as Pius XII
described the Cold War) is "the *most* effective way" to maintain peace. Indeed the Council, having deferred to the authority and wisdom of these unnamed "many" individuals,
then proceeds to list the dangers inherent in the arms race.

Those dangers, as viewed by Vatican II, include the following:

1. The "arms race ... is not a safe way to preserve a steady
peace."

2. The "balance resulting from this race" makes "the
causes of war threaten to grow gradually stronger."

3. The arms race does not produce the healing of "disagreements between nations" but "on the contrary other
parts of the world are infected with them."

4. The "arms race is an utterly treacherous trap for
humanity, and one which injures the poor to an intolerable
degree."

Despite its condemnation of the possession of massive armaments, the Council specifically states that it is *not* calling
for "a unilateral disarmament" but a disarmament "proceeding at an equal pace according to agreement." Once again
Vatican II appears to have recognized all the terrors and the
inherent futility of the massive mutual deterrence employed
by Russia and the United States, but then to have stepped
back from anything except the customary talk about mutually
agreed-upon disarmament.

One reasonable interpretation of Vatican II would be that
the Council fathers sought without notable success to reconcile the irreconcilable. The twenty-two hundred bishops of
the world felt compelled to join in "the condemnations of
total war already pronounced by recent popes." But then
they were unable or unwilling even to try to reconcile those
condemnations with the Council's acquiescence in, and even
acceptance of, the morality of the possession of nuclear
weapons whose only purpose is to destroy "entire cities or
extensive areas."

Vatican II, consequently, is left in the position of refusing
to condemn the possession of nuclear weapons when such
possession is retained as a method of deterrence. The Council, at least by implication, has thus stated that the evil of

bombing cities (which may never be carried out) may nonetheless be threatened. As a result of this basic contradiction in the twenty-five hundred words of Vatican II on modern war, it has to be said that the Council evaded the central and crucial issue related to modern war: the morality of the possession of nuclear arms retained as a method of deterrence.

One can, of course, argue that it would have been unrealistic for Vatican II to declare that the mere possession of modern arms whose only purpose is mass destruction is inherently immoral. Such a declaration would have made "sinners" out of most of the nations in the civilized world. The United States and Russia would have been the principal "sinners" because of their being willing, if necessary, to destroy "entire cities or extensive areas" and thus commit an act which the Vatican Council described as "a crime against God and man himself."

Vatican II therefore said nothing about the morality of armed deterrence as that concept has been understood and practiced during the twenty-five years of the Cold War. There can be little debate that the question of the morality of massive deterrence is the most important moral dilemma of the age and consequently the most urgent moral issue which confronted Vatican II. It is therefore distressing that Vatican II's response is so ambiguous and so contradictory.

There is, however, one significant and perhaps monumental development in Vatican II's position on war. This development is in the severity of the language with which the Council proscribed "any act of war aimed indiscriminately" at the destruction of cities or extensive areas. The word employed is "condemnation," a term seldom used in any of the sixteen constitutions, decrees, and declarations—running to some 103,000 words—issued by Vatican II.

There has been some dispute among scholars as to the ultimate reason and rationale for this condemnation.[1] Did

Vatican II issue its condemnation because it desired to absolutize the principle of the moral immunity of noncombatants from direct attack? Or did Vatican II mean to say that the destruction of cities, even if undertaken as an allegedly necessary military strategy, would violate the necessity of proportionality required before any war can be "just"? Or did the Council fathers feel that the obliteration of cities or extensive areas, along with their population, came under the Council's ban on genocide?

No one can establish with certainty which one or more of these principles led to the Council's unequivocal "condemnation." But the issuance of such a condemnation is nonetheless a new emphasis in Catholic thinking on war which, sooner rather than later, may be pushed to the limits of its logic by moralists and jurists.

Vatican II, almost contrary to its own hopes and intuitions, appears to have reaffirmed the traditional criteria for a just war. Those norms, originated by St. Augustine, refined by Aquinas, and synthesized by Vittoria, can be summarized as follows:

1. The war must be declared by a legitimate public authority possessing the power to do so;
2. a real injury must have been suffered;
3. the damage likely to follow from the war cannot be disproportionate to the injury suffered;
4. there must be a reasonable hope of success;
5. every possible means of peaceful settlement must have been exhausted;
6. those prosecuting the war must have a moral intention;
7. only legitimate and moral means may be utilized in prosecuting the war.[2]

Vatican II did not specify whether one or more or all of these criteria must be looked at "with an entirely new attitude." But at least Vatican II cast the most serious doubts on the continued validity and viability of the very notion of a "just" war.

It is the thesis of this book that the existence of nuclear arms and the possession by the United States and by Russia of fantastically destructive biological and chemical weapons make the possibility of a "just" war so remote that the Church could and should condemn war as morally objectionable.

It is also the thesis of this book that Vatican II's twenty-five hundred words on the morality of war are so unsatisfactory that a new ecumenical Council of all the bishops of the world (accompanied by lay leaders) should be convened as soon as possible and its agenda restricted to the single topic of war. Clearly no global problem has more overwhelming moral importance to mankind than the possibility of a nuclear war, or one in which biological and chemical weapons would be employed.

Notes

1. *See* Robert W. Tucker, *Just War and Vatican Council II: A Critique*, with commentary by George G. Higgins, Ralph Potter, Richard H. Cox, and Paul Ramsey (New York: Council on Religion and International Affairs, 1966).

2. For an exposition of the history of the traditional Catholic approach to war, *see* Heinrich A. Rommen, *The State in Catholic Thought* (St. Louis: B. Herder Book Co., 1945).

2.

The American Hierarchy and Vietnam: 1966

THERE ARE several important reasons why the more than two hundred Catholic bishops in America could have been expected to give more guidance and leadership on the Vietnam war than they did. The United States government was, after all, the major architect of the policy of the containment of communism by armed force. And Vietnam was the first instance in which the American government had made a decision to carry out by war its "commitment" to a nation in Southeast Asia. Somehow the same United States government had not felt obliged to repel the Communists in Cuba, ninety miles off the Florida coast, nor had it allowed itself to become involved in Hungary in 1956 or the Suez-Middle East crisis in the same year.

Korea, moreover, was distinguishable from Vietnam. In Korea the United States had some type of a mandate from the United Nations and hence did not act unilaterally as it did in Vietnam.

Despite these reasons, Catholics and Catholic bishops in America should have been intensely concerned about the morality of intervention in Vietnam. The United States was the first power to push through the research needed to develop the atomic bomb and the only nation to have had the recklessness to drop it. Clearly, the Vietnam struggle in November 1966, when the Catholic bishops of America spoke out for the first time, was capable of developing into a nuclear war.

Still another reason why the Catholic bishops might have spoken clearly and boldly was the stimulus given to searchers for peace everywhere by the strong if not entirely satisfactory words on war which Vatican II issued in the late fall of 1965. The American bishops, constituting some 10 percent of Vatican II, could hopefully have developed the beginnings made by Vatican II.

In view of all these events, the American hierarchy's statement in November 1966 can only be classified as a bitter disappointment. (See Appendix D.) Indeed this statement, coupled with the bishops' statement on the war in November 1968, have been held up as reasons why the present system of appointing bishops is inherently wrong. When Catholics as never before wanted guidance on peace and war, a group of good and pious men, appointed by Rome to be bishops and "safe" administrators, revealed their intellectual and spiritual bankruptcy.

It seems almost needless to review the contradictory statements issued by the bishops in November 1966, when the whole nation—and especially its youth—was torn apart by the agony and anguish of seeing daily on television American soldiers killing fellowmen in the nation's land war in Asia. The bishops' response (stripped of its rhetoric) was that "it is reasonable to argue that our presence in Vietnam is justified."

I recall well a cynical but profoundly Christian student saying to me the day after the bishops made their statement in 1966: "I gather that the bishops think it an act of virtue to follow the body count each day, since they say that 'our presence in Vietnam is justified.'"

It was, of course, widely disputed at that time whether the United States government could even offer a respectable *legal* argument for its presence in Vietnam. The bishops' bland statement (after almost absurdly conceding that they could not "resolve these issues authoritatively") that the war was "justified" outraged millions of young Catholics and alienated further millions of non-Catholics. If the collective statements of the American bishops ever had any significant influence or credibility, their believability went down after their first statement on the war in Vietnam.

What made the 1966 episcopal statement even worse was this pretentious and almost hypocritical statement:

> To the strong words of the National Council of Churches, the Synagogue Council of America, and other religious bodies, we add our own plea for peace. Our approaches may at times differ but our starting point (justice) and our goal (peace) do not.

There must have been an "approach" employed by the bishops, somewhere between their "starting point" and their "goal," which was fundamentally different from the Protestant and Jewish approach, because the bishops come out as "hawks" whereas the other groups with whom they claim harmony end up with almost entirely different conclusions.

A further limitation of the hierarchy's 1966 statement is the unfortunate way in which it begs the question on some crucial issues. The document asserts, for example, that since a "government cannot be denied the right to legitimate defense," it follows that "what a nation can do to defend itself, it may do to help another in its struggles against aggression." Such a statement, which sounds as if it were lifted from some handbook on moral theology, begs the central moral question in America's foreign policy: Can the United States enter a war to protect the territorial integrity of a far weaker, nonindustrialized nation when it is clear that such an intervention will turn that country into a battlefield between the nuclear powers of the world?

It may be suggested that it is unfair to level such criticism at the American bishops, since in November 1966 they could not be expected to be less confused or bewildered than other Americans with respect to the then rapidly escalating war in Vietnam. This suggestion undoubtedly has merit but it is the premises and presuppositions of the bishops which I wish to question as much as their conclusions. These premises go to the heart of the question of what the Christian's attitude should be when the state declares that it is necessary in the name of national safety to violate God's command, "Thou shalt not kill." Catholic tradition in America has, it seems to me, followed the line of least resistance in this area, and in so doing has been unfaithful to genuine Catholic teaching on the subject of war.

The hierarchy's statement of 1966 resolves, at least by implication, too many doubts in favor of a government (or, more accurately, a president), which has decided that some men must die. The bishops state naively that "Americans can have confidence in the sincerity of their leaders as long as they work for a just peace in Vietnam." The bishops further state that the government's "efforts to find a solution to the present impasse are well known." The implausibility of these two sentences prompts the bishops to state that "we realize that citizens of all faiths and of differing political loyalties honestly differ among themselves over the moral issues involved in this tragic conflict."

Despite this admitted nationwide dissent from the government's war policy, the bishops nonetheless affirm that "we can conscientiously support the position of our country in the present circumstances. . . ." Such a position makes little if any effort really to apply the definition of a just war to the situation in Vietnam. It does not even try to assess whether war was the only possible alternative left or whether more, or at least equal, good would predictably come from the war. In short the bishops' statement in 1966 appears to presume that one cannot fault the judgment made by officials in the White House and the Pentagon that an exception can be made to God's law against killing.

I am not, of course, stating that the bishops were erroneous in 1966 because they did not turn up with a dove position. On the contrary I am saying that their document, which is a collection of almost unrelated paragraphs, does not present a reasoned application of the Catholic theory of a just war; it appears to concede to the state too broad a power to determine those circumstances in which the life of human beings may be taken in the name of a less precious good such as an alleged threat to national safety.

The bishops' statement lags far behind European Catholic debate on the morality of war. Much of the stimulus for the widespread, generally antiwar Catholic thought on the Continent comes from the uncomfortable realization that in World War II most German Catholics resigned themselves to unquestioning service in the Nazi armies while Catholics on the Allied side cooperated without compunction in the ghastly slaughter of thousands of noncombatant civilians.

This European Catholic thought about war has received added stimulus from the mandate of Vatican II that Christians must look upon war with "an entirely new attitude." That new attitude should mean at least that a modern secular state has the burden of proving the justice of a particular war against the general presumption of the injustice of all wars. On this basis the American bishops, who complained in their statement about the lack of clear information about the war in Vietnam, could surely have stated that they had insufficient information to make a statement which would justify an action ordered by the government against the overriding authority of the Fifth Commandment.

A remarkable reply to the message of the National Conference of Catholic Bishops was issued by the Washington chapter of the Catholic Peace Fellowship. It is probably unprecedented as a rebuke to the American hierarchy from members of a Catholic organization. The content and the obvious anguish of this statement make it worthy of full reproduction:

> We greet the Statement of the National Conference of Catholic Bishops on Peace with genuine anguish. We greatly admire the Second Vatican Council's teaching on the principles of conscientious objectors; its demand for a universal public authority; its condemnation of "any act of war aimed indiscriminately at the destruction of ... extensive areas"; and its reminder that the means of waging war must be limited by moral considerations.
>
> When you, the bishops of the United States, sought to apply these principles, we anticipated a clear analysis of the Vietnam situation as well as a strong condemnation of the doubtful morality of aspects of that struggle.
>
> Instead, when we received your statement, we read that you "can conscientiously support the position of our country. ..."
>
> No outline of that position was given; no comment on the justice of the entire war nor the morality of particular aspects of it; no consideration of napalm bombing or crop poisoning, or the unusually high ratio of civilian casualties, or of whether the war is truly one of self-defense. Catholics are left as before to speak their own objections to savagery without the support of their spiritual leaders.
>
> Instead the impression has been undeniably given that you have examined the war, and have found the position of the United States to be just—that you can conscientiously support that position. And if you say that you have not given a blanket endorsement of that war, then we must ask: Why did you not emphasize as strongly and as clearly that this war can be

conscientiously opposed as well as conscientiously supported?

You came close to answering this question when you observe: "Citizens of all faiths and differing political loyalties honestly differ among themselves on the moral issues involved in this tragic conflict." Then recognizing these honest differences, you apparently gave your support on only one side. Sympathy goes to American leaders, but not to the Vietnamese people; reason is assigned to those who argue in favor of American presence in Vietnam, but not to those who argue against it; you commend the valor of men in the armed forces, but not those who suffer in prison because they refuse to participate in a war they believe immoral and unjust.

We know that it was not your intention to undercut opposition to the war or to negate the dictates of free conscience, but your statement is so misleading that you have done just this. Your support for the war is accompanied by qualifications, but you have so underemphasized those qualifications that they are being forgotten. The only way to prevent your statement from being misunderstood and misused is to frame another—one which specifies the moral limits of this war, one which supports conscientious objections to specific wars, and finally one which calls on both sides to "stop—even at the expense of some inconvenience or loss." [Pope Paul's October Letter on Peace].

We beg of you in the name of the suffering world to make such a statement.

3.

The American Hierarchy on War and Peace: 1968

AFTER AN UNEXPLAINED SILENCE in 1967 about the war in Vietnam, the American bishops issued a rather remarkable five-thousand-word statement on war and peace in November 1968. This document (reproduced in Appendix E) may possibly have great historic significance. It places the American bishops on record for the first time on some crucial issues such as conscientious objection to war, arms control, and peacetime military conscription.

The nagging question which recurs as one ponders the episcopal statement of 1968 is this: If a person concedes the morality of the possession of nuclear arms for defensive purposes, is there then any set of moral principles which have any real relevance and applicability to actual situations in the world of power politics?

The bishops, for example, stated in 1968 that "we seriously

question whether the present policy of maintaining nuclear superiority is meaningful for security." But they did not condemn the possession of nuclear warheads. Referring to the ABM system the bishops expressed the view that the U.S. decision to build an antiballistic missile system was America's "latest act in the continuing nuclear arms race," that such an action would upset "the present strategic balance" and would "incite other nations to increase their offensive nuclear forces."

This rather categorical condemnation of the ABM did not appear to be a significant factor in the national discussion and controversy which ended in the approval of the deployment of the ABM by the United States Senate on August 6, 1969, the twenty-fourth anniversary of America's atomic bombing of Nagasaki and Hiroshima. Nor did the bishops clearly state after the action of the Senate that their recommendation had been rejected. A statement to that effect by Monsignor Marvin Bordelon, the bishops' spokesman on matters of world peace, received routine coverage in the Catholic but not the daily press.

It therefore seems fair to say that if a person agrees not to condemn the policy of armed deterrence predicated on the capability of instant and massive retaliation, he does not have very much moral power when he urges that the present levels of armed preparedness not be increased. It would consequently appear to be unrealistic to expect that the more than two hundred Catholic bishops in America will be very persuasive to anyone as long as their position accepts—however reluctantly—what they themselves called the "balance of terror."

An implicit acknowledgment of the failure, or even of the inability, of the Catholic Church to form the consciences of Catholics on war is contained in the bishops' admission that, with regard to "the moral aspect of our involvement in Vietnam . . . opinions among Catholics appear as varied as in our society as a whole." Assuming that this statement is correct, the following inferences are possible:

1. There is nothing in Catholic teaching which would assist Catholics to come to an informed judgment about the morality of any modern war or at least about the war in Vietnam.

2. Whatever wisdom the highly developed Catholic theory of the just war might have had in the past, it has been lost or at least has not been communicated to American Catholics.

3. War today is a matter of "realpolitik" on which Catholics have no moral principles which differentiate them from other citizens.

Incredible as it may seem, the third inference seems to be the one followed by the bishops. They seek to interpret the lack of any particular viewpoint on the war in Vietnam among Catholics as a healthy phenomenon. They write that "one cannot accuse Catholics of either being partisans of any one point of view or of being unconcerned." After thus turning what many would call shame into glory, the bishops endorse "the fundamental right of political dissent" and encourage "rational debate on public policy decisions of government in the light of moral and political principles."

Despite this astonishing or perhaps only incomprehensible treatment of the alleged state of opinion among the nation's forty-six million Catholics, the bishops' statement contains some principles which are almost certainly in advance of many of the attitudes about war commonly held by Catholics in America. Among such views are the following:

1. American Catholics have the most serious obligation to give "moral leadership" to the world on the issue of peace because they live in a nation "whose arsenals contain the greatest nuclear potential."

2. All "wars of aggression" are condemned "without qualification." A case for such a war "can no longer be imagined, given the circumstances of modern warfare."

3. There should be "a total review of the draft system and the establishment of voluntary military service in a professional army." The bishops call "for the end of *any* draft system at home" (emphasis added).

4. One of the "moral lessons to be learned from our involvement in Vietnam" is the fact that "military power and technology do not suffice, even with the strongest resolve, to restore order and accomplish peace."

The presence of these forward-looking recommendations does not, however, save the bishops' 1968 statement from basic incoherence. The incoherence is the same as that in Vatican II. It derives from the fact that Vatican II, as interpreted by the American bishops, "did not call for unilateral disarmament." The bishops seek to justify this position by stating that "Christian morality is not lacking in realism." The concept of "realism" can, of course, cover all the sins and selfishness of men and nations who seek to retain power and territory by the employment of as much deadly force as is necessary. The truth is that today "realism" demands that moral principles be enunciated to prevent the imminent destruction of half of humanity. Unilateral disarmament may not prevent such a disaster. But the practical proscription of unilateral disarmament by Vatican II and by the American bishops, in the name of a "Christian morality" based on "realism," gives a certain indirect sanction to the continuation—and the inevitable escalation—of massive armaments by the Soviet and the American blocs.

There is a persuasive case for the proposition that the Church can never tailor its moral judgments so that they will not be criticized as "lacking in realism." At least when the Church is interpreting the Fifth Commandment, any exceptions permitted to the absolute rule of "Thou shalt not kill" cannot, under any norm of morality, law, or logic, be affected by the "realism" of a world where men and nations take lives in order to safeguard their own property or territory. In its

condemnation of duelling the Church did not try to enunciate a judgment which would be in accord with "realism." Nor
has the Church done so in its position on abortion, even
though—as we are reminded incessantly—pregnant women
who desire to terminate their pregnancy *will* find a way to
obtain an abortion, and therefore, as the argument goes, the
Church should be "realistic."

Toward the end of the 1968 statement the bishops seem
to be seeking a way out of the cul-de-sac caused by their
toleration of the possession of massive armaments. They seek
this way out by an attempt to apply the norm of proportionality to the war in Vietnam. But the questions about proportionality which the episcopal statement raises and cannot resolve
seem to demonstrate that even this norm, possibly the most
helpful of all the tests included in the just war theory, has no
real validity or viability when applied to a modern war. Even
if one assumes, as the bishops do, that the proportionality test
is helpful, it breaks down almost immediately when applied
to Vietnam. Who will say that the preservation of the political
independence of one-half of a nation from its other half can
justify thousands of deaths, the destruction of millions of
food-producing acres, and the festering of the social problems of the poor in America to the point of revolution?

Indeed the studied ambiguity of the questions about proportionality in the bishops' statement, and the total absence
of any attempt at answering them, more than suggest that the
bishops themselves seemed uncertain as to whether the principle still has any usefulness. They ask whether the conflict
in Vietnam has "provoked inhuman dimensions of suffering"
without, however, even attempting to set forth any norms by
which the dimensions of such suffering can be measured
against the principle of proportionality.

Although the 1968 message of the Catholic bishops on
peace and war is probably the best statement ever made by
that group on the subject of war, the statement nonetheless

appears to assume that the abolition of war is not foreseeable and that all of us should recognize that "war remains a melancholy fact of life today."

The foregoing review of what the Catholic bishops in America have said about the cruelest and most controversial war in American history suggests the question whether anyone had a right to expect more than has been received from this source. In all candor the historical fact is, as E. I. Watkin has brought out, that "bishops have consistently supported all wars waged by the government of their country."[1] Watkin adds that he does not know "of a single instance in which a national hierarchy has condemned as unjust any war, however patently an unjust aggression, declared by such a government." Watkin points out further that nationalism inhibited the European hierarchies from supporting Pope Benedict XV's attempts during World War I to secure a negotiated peace—an event which would have prevented the death and dispossession of millions of persons.

It seems clear that a misconceived patriotism, a basic uncertainty about the Church's position on war, and a sense of futility in speaking out against war have all combined to silence the highest national representatives of a supranational Church.

The issue is, to be sure, difficult and excruciating. In the year 1139, for example, Pope Innocent II presided over Lateran Council II, the tenth ecumenical council in the history of the Church. A canon enacted by this supremely authoritative organ of the Church forbade as immoral the employment in warfare of bows and arrows. The rulers of Western Europe, all Catholics, simply ignored this decree. In fact they did not even bother to protest its existence. A pious commentator, as Mr. Watkin has brought out in the essay noted above, has tried to save the face of Catholic obedience by the unsupportable suggestion that the decree of Lateran II condemned archery only in private armed conflict rather than in warfare between nations.

The grim fact is that all of the attempts of the Church to civilize warfare have gone unheeded, at least in the long range of history. Medieval movements, such as the Peace of God, were, to be sure, successful in mitigating the terrible effects of unlimited warfare.[2] But the Church's position on war as such has always remained ambivalent. In 1179, for example, at the Third Lateran Council, Pope Alexander III gave papal recognition and approval to the decrees of French and Spanish episcopal councils which had placed various classes of the civilian population beyond the range of ethically permissible military attack.

As one reads the history of the Church's frustrations in seeking to mitigate the atrocities of war, there comes to mind the statement of Justice Benjamin Cardozo that people will seize upon every concession in a law and push it to the limit of its logic. Is it possible that the mere existence of *some* permission by the Church to wage war has allowed Christian men to justify in their consciences what their minds indicate to them is the fulfillment of the Cain-instinct?

What would be the status of war in Christendom today, if the Church had retained through the centuries the antiwar sentiment which characterized Christianity in its first three centuries prior to the Edict of Constantine? Is war so pervasive an instinct of mankind that it is unrealistic to expect that even the severest sanctions against it by the Church would be sufficient to eliminate it? If the *ecclesia docens,* the teaching Church, today enunciated in-season and out-of-season the almost pacifist attitudes of the pre-Constantine church, would the *ecclesia credens,* the believing Church, accept and follow it?

Clearly there is an opportunity, a challenge, and a mandate of this time for both the hierarchy and the laity to rethink their position on war. It was, as we can never recall frequently enough, "an *entirely* new attitude" on war which Vatican II demanded.

It seems fair to state that the silence or the ineffectiveness of the Church through the centuries has allowed wars to increase in number and savagery. In the first thousand years of the Christian era, as the expert on morality and war, Father Francis Stratmann, O.P. has written, "numerous ecclesiastical synods imposed severe penances on killing in war."[3] The Crusades brought a change. For the first time the Church was openly advocating the attainment of a presumably spiritual objective by armed conflict. Some of the Crusades "degenerated into senseless bloodshed," and the "net gain for the Kingdom of God was nil."[4]

Nowhere does there appear to be a satisfactory or scholarly justification of the use of war in the Crusades.[5] At the same time few Catholic scholars have described the Crusades as the source of the impetus to war which came into Western Europe during the second millennium of Christianity. It may be, however, that the harnessing of military power for religious objectives, first witnessed on any large scale in the Christian era in the Crusades, weakened the credibility of the Church to such an extent that the Church could no longer teach very effectively that killing in a war is justified only in the most extraordinary instance and after *every* other *possible* remedy had been attempted.

Whatever the complex causes for the recurring presence and the escalating horrors of war in the Christian West, it is humiliating for a Christian to have to admit that wars—probably more numerous or at least more savage than any in recorded history—have been undertaken by nations where the Gospel of Love is followed by the vast majority of people.

The American bishops, writing in 1966 and 1968, knew all these grim facts. In November 1968 they wrote their statement after a massive protest against the war in Vietnam had torn the American nation asunder, had toppled an incumbent president, and had been the critical issue in the then recently concluded presidential election. The bishops issued an excellent, moving, and very valuable document.

That document, however, evaded the ultimate and, in the final analysis, the only important moral question: If America's foreign policy of threatened massive retaliation against her potential enemies is illusory and immoral because these weapons, as Vatican II made clear beyond any doubt, may never be employed, how then can Catholics in America continue to be employed in the manufacture, handling, and planned deployment of those weapons?

The question is so new and so startling that almost everyone will dismiss it as pacifist in orientation, unrealistic in practice, and absurd in its consequences. But in fact it is the question on which the Church has been hedging for a long time. The reluctance of the Church to speak to the issue has been more obvious and more scandalous since the nuclear age began in 1945.

Bishops, probably in the same proportion as laymen, would say that the issues are not clear enough to forbid the cooperation of Catholics in the manufacture and use of weapons whose inevitable effect, if not their stated intention, is to kill innocent noncombatants. Others would say quite correctly that millions of Catholics would not obey and hence the numbers of the faithful would be reduced to a handful.

If those lines of reasoning persist, Catholics will not have as a matter of practice any views on war different from non-Catholics or non-Christians. This, it must be said, is probably the actual state of things today.

One of the reasons why the material in Vatican II on war and the American bishops' statement in 1968 are not entirely satisfactory derives from a limitation they have in common. That limitation arises from the fact that each was issued as part of a longer and very important document, and both—for a variety of reasons—received insufficient attention from their authors.

Although the issue of war did not receive attention at Vatican II until the third session, an unofficial eleven-point schema concerning peace was circulated among the Council fathers in the closing days of the first session.[6] One of the points in the proposed conciliar statement (on which Cardinal Maurice Feltin, archbishop of Paris, looked with favor) was a recommendation that "today, any war would bring about evils infinitely greater than those it would pretend to abolish."[7] There is no record that the bishops of Vatican II gave to this proposition the full consideration which it merits.

The history of Vatican II also suggests that at the third and final sessions of the Council a large number of issues prevented a full discussion of the subject of peace and war. The attempt of six American prelates to introduce an intervention designed to weaken the Council's condemnation of nuclear war[8] prevented the Council from hearing the "many in the Council who wished to declare unilateral disarmament as obligatory."[9]

In the following chapter we will take up the question of whether Vatican II's statement on war failed to follow the lead of the remarkable message which Pope John issued in *Pacem in Terris* on Easter Sunday in 1963. Certainly the encyclical had little, if any, influence on the 1968 statement of the American bishops.

The first part of the bishops' message, to which they gave most of their attention, was an explication of *Humanae Vitae.* It may be, of course, that if the bishops had had more time to consider the implications of the most important words on war of the Catholic hierarchy in American history, those six prelates, who had urged the participants in Vatican II to drop its condemnation of nuclear arms because "there is still no consensus of opinion among theologians,"[10] might have persuaded their brother bishops to weaken the American hierarchy's position. In any event neither Vatican II nor the American bishops have really faced the agonizing dilemmas of modern war.

We turn now to an evaluation of *Pacem in Terris* and to this question: Did Vatican II and the American bishops overlook or reject Pope John's approach to war as enunciated in *Pacem in Terris?*

Notes

1. In Charles S. Thompson, ed., *Morals and Missiles* (New York: Oxford University Press, 1960).

2. *See* Maurice Keen, *The Laws of War in the Late Middle Ages* (Toronto: University of Toronto Press, 1965). *See also* Walter Ullman, *The Medieval Idea of Law as Represented by Lucas de Penna* (London: Oxford University Press, 1946).

3. In Thompson, *op. cit.*, p. 19.

4. *Ibid.*

5. *The New Catholic Encyclopedia* (New York: McGraw-Hill Book Company, 1967), vol. 4, p. 511. *See also* related articles on the Crusades.

6. Vincent A. Yzermans, ed., *American Participation in the Second Vatican Council* (New York: Sheed and Ward, 1967), pp. 215-221.

7. *Ibid.*, p. 215.

8. *Ibid.*, pp. 216-219.

9. *Ibid.*, p. 219.

10. *Ibid.*, p. 220.

4.

Pacem in Terris:
The Morality of War

Pacem in Terris was greeted by the entire world with more exultant joy than any other papal message within living memory. A part or even most of the reaction was attributable to the incredible and incomprehensible love affair which the world still enjoys with its author, Pope John XXIII.

This last encyclical of Pope John's is proof of many things, but above all it perhaps demonstrates that Gandhi was correct when he said that "human nature is one and therefore unfailingly responds to the advances of love."[1]

The sections of *Pacem in Terris* devoted to peace and war certainly shift the emphasis away from that spirit of militant anticommunism so manifest in the pronouncements of Pius XI and Pius XII. Pope John pleaded for mediation and not militancy, for world peace and not for a world campaign against communism. He stated that "nuclear weapons should be banned. ... It is hardly possible to imagine that in the

atomic era war could be used as an instrument of justice."
He urged, furthermore, that

> All must realize that there is no hope of putting an end to the
> building up of armaments, nor of reducing the present stocks,
> nor, still less, of abolishing them altogether, unless the process
> is complete and thorough, and unless it proceeds from inner
> convictions. ...

The idealism and near-naivete of *Pacem in Terris* is evident from the entire tone of the encyclical as well as from the
fact, for example, that only twice does it refer to the sinfulness of man which has introduced ever more heinous forms
of war into every generation. But the loftiness of *Pacem in
Terris* was apparently the very element which prompted fa-
vorable and enthusiastic comments from Soviet Premier
Nikita Khruschev, President John Kennedy, U Thant, and
almost every well-known Protestant and Jewish theologian.[2]
The pope's message, with its appeal to the entire world to
"banish the fear and anxious expectation of war with which
men are oppressed," reached and touched the deepest hopes
and fears of all mankind.

But after all the applause for *Pacem in Terris* (and it continued through 1965),[3] one must ask the hard question: Did
this document in 1963 enunciate principles about peace and
war which were overlooked or rejected by Vatican II in 1965
and by the American bishops in 1968?

My answer is Yes.

The first insight which *Pacem in Terris* stressed, but which
was inadequately reflected in Vatican II and in the statement
of the American bishops, was Pope John's admonition that
the Russians and Communists throughout the world must
realize that their doom is inevitable if they dare to activate
their first-strike capability through the use of nuclear weapons.

The pope, however, seemed hopeful that his warning was

unnecessary, for he clearly assumed that there was a good measure of humane instincts residing in communist leaders. Others did not share his optimism; they criticized his assumption as an unrealistic and naive concept.[4] But George F. Kennan, the international expert on Russia and communism, in his address at the 1965 International Conference on *Pacem in Terris,* appeared to endorse Pope John's views. He echoes the pope's fear of fear when he states that East-West relations cannot improve so long as there exists "an atmosphere of pervasive suspicion and fear—particularly fear addressed to the inconceivable disasters of a war conducted with nuclear weapons."[5] Kennan goes on to reinforce Pope John's rejection of the sterile stereotypes which have poisoned East-West relations during all of the years of the Cold War. Kennan writes:

> ... I should like to plead for a basis revision of assumptions concerning Soviet intentions, both hypothetical and actual. Western policy is apparently based on an assessment of these intentions which has not changed appreciably from the days of the Berlin blockade and the Korean war, and which, even then, probably embraced serious elements of misinterpretation.[6]

These assumptions, Kennan adds, cannot "be reconciled ... with communist doctrine ... nor with the present state of relations between Moscow and the communist countries of Eastern Europe." In a point directly reaffirming Pope John's view of the leaders in Moscow, Kennan states that the assumption held by persons in Western countries "impute to the Soviet leaders a total inhumanity not plausible even in nature and out of accord with those human ideals we must recognize as lying ... at the origins of all European Marxism."[7]

Finally Kennan practically restates Pope John's thesis with a plea "for something resembling a *new act of faith* in the *ultimate humanity* and sobriety of the people on the other side"[8] (emphasis added). Kennan supports this appeal with the penetrating reminder that "the penalties for overcynicism in the estimation of motives of others can be no smaller, on occasions, than the penalties for naivete."[9] Only by remembering these truths, Kennan says, can men approach that state of mutual trust which *Pacem in Terris* reminds the world "is something which reason requires . . . is eminently desirable in itself and . . . will prove to be the source of many benefits."

If *Pacem in Terris* had been written by anyone except Pope John, its author would almost certainly have been rebuked by hard-line anti-Soviets as "soft" on communism. Professor Paul Ramsey has described the approach and tone of *Pacem in Terris* as that of a "liberal Protestant preacher."[10] But in the vast outpouring of commentary on the encyclical there appears to be no solidly reasoned rejection of Pope John's view of the Communists. To be sure John Courtney Murray, S.J., suggested that Pope John's "spirit of confident hope" may arguably fail "to take realistic account of the fundamental schism in the world today."[11] Reinhold Niebuhr, the eminent Protestant theologian, felt that the pope had failed "to consider the problems of immediate security that confront both sides of the horrible nuclear dilemma. . . . This idealism is a little too easy."[12] Will Herberg detected "a pervasive confusion of perspective"[13] in *Pacem in Terris.* But not even the harshest critics of the encyclical said that Pope John's view of communist intentions was not plausible.

One's attitude with respect to the intentions of Russia would appear at first not to depend on any theological or religious viewpoint. On reconsideration, however, it seems clear that the deep faith and profound love with permeates *Pacem in Terris* alters Pope John's view of what evil the Communists might initiate. How precisely his judgments of the present-day predicament are altered by faith and love is not easy to pinpoint. It is rather the mood, the tone, and the approach of *Pacem in Terris* which make it different from the subsequent pronouncements of Vatican II and the American bishops. Some might say that at Easter of 1963 Pope John witnessed a quiet moment in the Cold War and thus did not have to confront, as did the bishops at Vatican II in December 1965, the massive military assistance given by Russian and Chinese Communists to the North Vietnamese. Nor did Pope John have to take into consideration, as the American bishops did in November 1968, the massive amount of arms furnished by Russia to the Arab nations, much of which was destroyed in the six-day Arab-Israeli war in June 1967.

The attitude that the Free World takes toward the Soviet empire at any given moment tends to reflect the most recent conduct of the Communists. There is, of course, a very good case for persistent and unrelenting resistance to the Communists. No one can deny the rapacity and the brutality of the Soviets in seizing control of the satellite nations in Eastern Europe in 1945 and retaining domination of them ever since that time. Nor can the hostility of the Peking government to the Free World be blinked at. But persistent hostility toward communism in all its forms is self-defeating. It may give the appearance of being the only logical and rational policy, but its inevitable effect is to deepen the antagonism of the Communists, intensify the Cold War, and escalate the arms race.

Can Christians who have deep faith and great love abate the hostility of the Communists simply by expressing trust in them, by recognizing their humanity, and by extending a hand of friendship? A great Christian, Pope John, did exactly that. The reaction was impressive but the real effect, if any, on communist policy cannot really be measured. Nor did the pope's example permeate Vatican II or alter the inflexible anticommunism of the American bishops, an attitude which is perhaps shared by the majority of American Catholics.

Dr. John C. Bennett noted that *Pacem in Terris* "calls Christians in the West away from the kind of anticommunism by which they have often been obsessed." He expressed the hope that since "American Catholicism seemed to give spiritual support to the kind of anticommunism that Pope John now opposes, his influence may have a profound effect on the Church in this country and through it upon the quality of American life."[14]

There are many reactions to the apparent failure of the Church to catch the spirit of reconciliation with communism which Pope John radiates in *Pacem in Terris*. Persons with the adamant "never-trust-the-Reds" approach treat *Pacem in Terris* as nothing but a pious prayer of a lovely man a few weeks before death. An articulate and reasoned "hawk," Professor William V. O'Brien, expressed the gap between Pope John's thinking and Catholics in general in these telling words:

> The pope's optimistic view of the prospects for greater under-standing with the Communists, his trust in an ever more pow-erful world organization which we must build on the basis of the United Nations, and his belief that the peace of the world is destined to rest, presumably in some foreseeable future, on trust rather than on fear, *are not really shared by most American Catholics*[15] (emphasis added).

The fact is that virtually no one who believes in America's foreign policy of containment shares Pope John's cautious optimism that the Cold War could be ended if both sides, or even one side, tried hard enough. America is now entering its second generation of pursuing a policy of possessing mas-sive armaments ready to be unleashed on a second-strike basis to carry out a threat of massive retaliation. Most Ameri-cans have succumbed to the psychological warfare carried on by the Pentagon and have become persuaded that it is neces-sary to spend almost $100 billion annually to protect the nation's security. Few persons realize that America has be-come a militaristic nation, as Gen. David Shoup (ret.) pointed out in a forceful article in the April 1969 *Atlantic Monthly*.

Undoubtedly munitions makers and the vast power of the
military perpetuate the idea of the indispensability of massive armaments because of the alleged irreversibility of the
Communists' designs. And political leaders, out of fear for
public opinion, are not able or willing to urge dialogue, disarmament, or even arms control. Indeed America really does
not want such an approach and the government does not
actually pursue such an objective. As Professor William
O'Brien puts it in his commentary on *Pacem in Terris:*

> ... in terms of budgetary appropriations, office space, man-
> hours, mobilized genius, knowledge, and intelligence, the
> efforts of the United States government are not really directed
> towards the immediate, early, or, I would contend, remotely
> foreseeable realization of those ultimate goals.[16]

The American people and the United States government
have been driven by ignorance, fear, and panic to the position that communism is an immutable movement which, according to its own inner logic, cannot be at peace with the
noncommunist world. Pope John denies this contention,
obliquely but clearly. He writes that sincere efforts at "peaceful adjustment" will lead to the discovery of "that point of
agreement from which it will be possible to commence to go
forward towards accords that will be sincere, lasting, and
fruitful."

Perhaps Pope John believed more than most Christians in
the efficacy of Paul's injunction to "disarm malice with kindness" (Romans 12:21). In any event he put forth, in a remarkable and brilliant way, several ideas about peace which were
not picked up by Vatican II or by the American bishops.
Pope John did not expressly repudiate the validity of the just
war theory, but the most quoted sentence of *Pacem in Terris*
is nevertheless the pope's assertion that "it is hardly possible
to imagine that in the atomic era war could be used as an
instrument of peace." If this statement does not quite reject

the just war theory, it suggests that the requirement of proportionality in the theory can seldom if ever be verified.

Whatever else *Pacem in Terris* might demonstrate, it offers overwhelming proof that humanity today, agonizing over the fantastic scientific powers it possesses to destroy human life, is desperate for some moral guidance in which hope and love are seen as the source of certainty and peace.

What are the principal ambiguities, contradictions, and omissions in all of the Catholic responses to war in the years of the atomic era—a period of unprecedented modernization in the Church? To that subject we now turn our attention.

Notes

1. James W. Douglass, *The Non-Violent Cross: A Theology of Revolution and Peace* (New York: The Macmillan Company, 1968), p. 86.

2. *See* "Pacem in Terris," *Worldview* (special issue) (June 1963).

3. *See* Edward Reed, ed., *Pacem in Terris—Peace on Earth* (New York: Pocket Books, Inc., 1965), the proceedings of an international convocation on "The Requirements of Peace," sponsored by the Center for the Study of Democratic Institutions.

4. *See* quotation of John F. Cronin, S. S., in Paul Ramsey, *The Just War: Force and Political Responsibility* (New York: Charles Scribner's Sons, 1968), p. 71.

5. Reed, *op. cit.*, note 3, p. 82.

6. *Ibid.*

7. *Ibid.*, pp. 82 ff.

8. *Ibid.*

9. *Ibid.*

10. Ramsey, *op. cit.*, pp. 71-62.

11. *America*, April 27, 1963.

12. *"Pacem in Terris," Christianity and Crisis*, May 13, 1963.

13. *"Pacem in Terris," National Review*, May 7, 1963.

14. "Peace on Earth," *Christianity and Crisis*, May 13, 1964.

15. "Balancing the Risks," *Worldview* (June 1963), pp. 10-11.

16. *Ibid.*, p. 10.

5.

Did the Just War Theory Die at the Birth of the Atomic Age?

BEFORE ATTEMPTING to clarify the ambiguities in the Church's position on war it should be carefully and clearly noted that the Catholic Church actually has no official "teaching" as such on war. There is, in other words, nothing in Scripture or tradition which the Church has taken and declared to be revealed. Nor is there even anything about war which is declared by the Church to be knowable from reason and which cannot be rejected by Catholics.

The traditional teaching by Catholic theologians on the subject of war may therefore be rejected if it is deemed to be erroneous or, as is more and more the case, if it is thought to be irrelevant because it is inapplicable.

It must also be pointed out that the traditional doctrine of theologians on war is a series of teachings which can only be classified as confused and so ambiguous that it is difficult to see how any application of it to even nonnuclear war would yield valuable results.

For example, in *Moral and Pastoral Theology* by Henry Davis, S.J., the just war is defined as always a war which is "defensive."[1] An "offensive war ... is always unjust."[2]

If, moreover, the "reasons for undertaking war are *not certainly just,* it is more generally taught that war may not be undertaken"[3] (emphasis added). Father Davis mentions the taking of property and the violation of national honor as reasons why wars happen, but gives no norms by which a nation is to judge whether their cause is "certainly just" and hence one which justifies war.

With regard to the moral obligations of soldiers, Father Davis is even more ambiguous. He states that "soldiers who are conscripted, or those who joined before the war, may usually presume that their country is in the right; in doubt they are bound to obey."[4] This way of resolving doubts, however, somehow does not apply to all participants in war since, Davis holds, "soldiers who freely join up after the war has begun must satisfy themselves that the cause is just."[5]

Father Davis is clear, however, on one thing; he states that "if the war is manifestly unjust, a soldier may not lawfully inflict any damage on the enemy. ..."[6] If Christian soldiers followed this norm, there would indeed be many conscientious objectors, since presumably these soldiers would also agree with Father Davis that "offensive war ... is always unjust."

While condoning defensive warfare, Father Davis declares nonetheless that "the fear of possible aggression by the enemy in the distant future is not a reason for ... subjugating ... a people"[7]—a principle which seems to have clear relevance to Vietnam and to other possible armed conflicts designed to prevent "possible aggression ... in the distant future."[8]

A careful inspection of the articles on war published in the *Catholic Encyclopedia* in 1913 and the *New Catholic Encyclopedia* published in 1967 reveals a disappointing lack of development in the intervening fifty years. The author of the 1967 article, Richard A. McCormick, S.J., a highly competent moral theologian, will not concede that the just war theory has been rendered obsolete or inapplicable by modern events. Struggling with a paucity of writing on the matter of war, Father McCormick uses as his principal support a 1959 article in *Theological Studies* by Father John Courtney Murray. This twenty-page piece, written about a subject relatively new to the author, is not one of Murray's better reasoned or original articles. Seeing a middle ground between "pacifism and bellicism," he vindicates the just war theory at least as a solvent of this dilemma, but ends by conceding that a new "politico-moral analysis" of modern war is needed.

The McCormick article does concede, however, that to some extent "there is no longer any just war theory, because these popes [Pius XII and John XXIII] have withdrawn the right of war in the situations to which these tests or conditions had references, i.e.," offensive war." Hence, Father McCormick concludes, there has been "a radical adjustment of traditional teaching on just warfare."[9] How such a "radical adjustment" differs from the abolition of the teaching is not clear. He also concedes that the "concept of aggression constitutes a problem in itself." It is without meaning from a military standpoint, since "aggression" is no longer the crossing of borders but "the use of enormous force from great distances."[10]

Though Father McCormick's article was written in 1966, it was not possible to incorporate into it what Vatican II had said about war in December 1965. In any case, it is not likely that very much would have been added.

Certainly, the history of the just war theory does not add

to its credibility. Despite the fact that St. Augustine had laid the foundations of the traditional teaching on the just war, severe penances were imposed by ecclesiastical synods during the 9th, 10th, and 11th centuries upon those who had shed blood in battle. This practice apparently derived from the the widespread conviction that killing in warfare was often done without justification and therefore deserved to be punished.[11]

Although wars of all kinds continued in Christian Europe through the centuries, moral theologians today would not in all likelihood disagree with a famous theologian who, around 1790, wrote that "war brings such evils with it—such harm to religion and to the innocent—that in practice it is *hardly ever* justifiable"[12] (emphasis added).

The just war concept is built on the notion of the sovereignty of the nation-state. Catholic theologians have conferred upon the nation-state rights and powers which, as one discovers in the manuals of ethics and moral theology, are frightening. The nation-state is said to be a "perfect society" which, like the Church, is autonomous and self-sufficient in its own sphere of competence. What is clearly lacking in almost every treatment of the modern state and its right to go to war is recognition of the fact that the rights of the family of nations have long since impinged on the rights of a single sovereign state.

The almost unbelievable array of rights conferred on this nation-state by Catholic theologians can be seen in the 1913 *Catholic Encyclopedia* article on war written by Charles Macksey, S.J., professor of ethics at the Gregorian University in Rome. He states that

> Catholic philosophy concedes to the State the full natural right of war, whether defensive, ... [or] offensive where it finds it necessary to take the initiative in the application of force; or punitive, in the infliction of punishment for evil done against itself. ...[13]

This author goes on to state that "international law views the punitive right of war with suspicion; but, though it is open to wide abuse, its original existence under the natural law cannot well be disputed."[14] As noted previously, Catholic teaching now proscribes all offensive wars and it would seem, a fortiori, punitive wars. Therefore the incredible assertion in 1913 by a professor at the Church's most prestigious seminary, that punitive war is a right granted to every nation by the natural law, tends to undermine the credibility of virtually everything which theologians have said about a nation's right to kill people to vindicate its claims or its honor.

In view of the foregoing, it is not surprising that Catholics in several nations are questioning whatever may be left of the just war theory. In Holland a Catholic writer, J. Arntz, has urged that the theory of the just war be stripped of its theological pretensions.[15] He seeks to demonstrate that this theory was originally nothing but an attempt to contain a war which in principle was hardly justifiable. This author feels that in the course of history the just war theory has not acted as a limitation on war but rather as an affirmation of the necessity of war.

In France Father Rene Coste, in his 1964 book, *Morale Internationale,* has sought to develop what he calls a "relative pacifism." Conceding that this solution will not satisfy either camp, Father Coste confesses that he is simply unable to deny that a nation has a right to defend itself in a non-atomic war. At the same time he advocates the development of spiritual resistance rather than armed defense by Christians whose government has been seized by an alien power. But Father Coste—like virtually all Catholic writers on the topic of war—does not meet head-on the claim of the pacifists that the radical love required by the New Testament makes it impossible to think that any war, particularly a modern war, could be an instrument of justice.

Also in France, where Catholics have been intensely active in peace movements, two symposia have searched the just war theory. *L'Atome pour ou contre l'homme,* published in 1958, has excellent historical documentation but demonstrates that any exploration of the just war theory along traditional lines seems painfully irrelevant. Also in 1958, in a special number of *Lumiere et Vie: Le chrétien et la guerre,* an outstanding article by D. Dubarle argues that the unification of the human community throughout the world no longer allows an appeal to the classical formulation of the just war theory. Dubarle cogently argues that modern nation-states lack that degree of independence and self-sufficiency which had been postulated by the traditional just war doctrine.

It seems increasingly clear that any attempt to accommodate the just war theory to contemporary conditions ends in unsatisfactory results. The theoretical discussion about this subject becomes so superfluous that people try to develop a practical attitude towards the seeming inevitability of war. In this connection, Cardinal Lercaro of Bologna said in May 1967 that the notion of a war for legitimate defense, which may possibly be a consensus among Catholics, "seems to be left over from cases and mental attitudes which no longer have anything to do with facts."[16]

As one discovers more and more about the Church's indecisiveness and waverings in past centuries about the morality of war, one becomes persuaded that the theory of a just war has never really been developed in any rational or coherent way. Perhaps theologians have become blinded or intimidated by nationalism. Or it may be that more precise standards to test the justice of the enormous complexities of warfare simply are not possible. But at least one major development seems to have occurred in the recent past: Offensive war has been condemned with such an unprecedented certainty and vehemence that the inner logic of this position may lead to the banning of all war.

Notes

1. (New York: Sheed and Ward, 1959), vol. II, p. 148.
2. *Ibid.*
3. *Ibid.*, pp. 151ff.
4. *Ibid.*
5. *Ibid.*
6. *Ibid.*
7. *Ibid.*
8. *Ibid.*
9. Vol. 14, pp. 354 ff.
10. *Ibid.*
11. *See* Walter Stein, ed., *Nuclear Weapons: A Catholic Response* (New York: Sheed and Ward, 1961), pp. 105-106.
12. *Ibid.*, p. 107.
13. (New York: The Encyclopedia Press, Inc., 1913), vol. XV, p. 108.
14. *Ibid.*, p. 109.
15. *See* Coenrad Van Ouwerkerk, C.SS.R., "War, Poverty and Freedom," *Concilium* 15.
16. James W. Douglass, *The Non-Violent Cross: A Theology of Revolution and Peace* (New York: The Macmillan Company, 1968), p. 178.

6.

Unresolved Problems:
Tyrannicide and Revolution

THE PERPETUATION of the conceptual framework of the just war theory has, it would appear, prevented innovative and creative approaches in the theology of a just war. The just war doctrine, for example, is grounded on the presumed dichotomy of offensive and defensive war. With the best of intentions, theologians—and apparently Vatican II—have now stated that an offensive war is never justified. But where does this leave the ethicist who desires to fashion some guidelines for the wars of a revolutionary and counterinsurgency nature which, for the foreseeable future, will be the principal type of armed conflict in the Third World where two-thirds of humanity reside? Whatever thought Catholic authorities have in this area can be reviewed by an analysis of the Church's views on tyrannicide and revolution.

Tyrannicide

If it were morally permissible to kill a ruler who had become
a tyrant, at least a few revolutions would be prevented. Moral
theologians through the centuries have been in total dis-
agreement about tyrannicide, although they have concurred
in the theory of the just war which would allow one nation
to kill the necessary number of nontyrants in another country.

St. Thomas Aquinas wrote that private individuals have a
tacit mandate from legitimate authority to kill a usurper when
no other means of ridding the community of the tyrant are
available.[1] However logical this theory may be—that is, if one
subscribes to the Thomistic theory of a just war—theologians
have rejected it.

In 1599 the Spanish Jesuit Mariana wrote a volume with
the thesis that people oppressed by a tyrant beyond the point
of duration should come together, warn the tyrannical ruler
of their intentions of killing him and, if this is to no avail, put
the tyrant to death. Although this book followed the teaching
of Aquinas, Suarez, and Bellarmine on tyrannicide and had
ecclesiastical approval in Spain, the Jesuit general Claudius
Acquaviva, withdrew the book from circulation in the year
1610 and forbade any member of the Jesuit order to teach
publicly or privately that it is lawful to attempt the life of a
tyrant.[2]

Alphonsus Ligouri later condemned any type of tyrannicide and "rejected as false and pernicious the opinions of
Suarez."[3]

The Church has never made any authoritative declaration
on the subject of tyrannicide but in 1913 Father J. M. Harty,
professor of moral theology and canon law at Maynooth
Seminary in Dublin, wrote as follows:

.... the Catholic doctrine condemns tyrannicide as opposed
to natural law [although] formerly great theologians like St.

Thomas, Suarez, Banez, O.P., permitted rebellion against op-
pressive rulers when the tyranny had become extreme and
when no other means of safety were available.[4]

Because Catholic writing on tyrannicide is almost nonex-
istent, one can only speculate on why theologians rejected
the viewpoint held by Aquinas, Suarez, Luther, and Me-
lanchthon—all of whom concurred in the teaching that the
people of a nation had a right to kill a tyrant when this was
the one way by which they could end the tyranny. Why did
Catholic theologians confer the right to wage offensive and
defensive wars against intolerable conditions upon rulers,
while withdrawing the right from the people of a nation to
wage war on an intolerable tyrant within their own nation?
Why did the right of tyrannicide appear moral to theologians
and Church leaders from at least the time of Aquinas until
close to the death of Suarez in 1617? Were Church officials
after this time so anxious to placate kings and rulers that they
systematically told theologians to "eliminate" the right to
tyrannicide?

The central question appears to be this: Why does the
nation-state alone have the right to decide what tyranny
justifies the death of human beings? If anyone is to be
granted the power to extinguish life in a morally justifiable
manner, why should the recipients of this right be only the
supreme rulers of the entity we call "nations"? Other entities
undoubtedly suffer far greater injustices than nations. Why
has the Church told them to suffer their misfortunes with
patience while the nation-state is granted the moral power to
kill in the name of the common good?

No one relishes the idea of spokesmen for the Church of
Christ permitting or justifying tyrannicide. But if they are to
sanction the extinction of the lives of "enemies" in a war,
then they should at least adopt the principle that a policy of
"permitting" deaths will be followed when such a policy

could conceivably eliminate the necessity of deaths to be caused by war.

It is inconsistent to permit the rulers of a nation to kill in a defensive war (to which the just war theory is now restricted) because of some injury to the nation's territory or property, while denying to the people of the nation the right to kill a real tyrant who has invaded all types of basic human and personal rights. Furthermore, it is reasonable to assume that the sanctioning of tyrannicide under carefully restricted conditions would diminish the number of wars and cause rulers to be more responsive to their people.

If a pious reader may wonder whether I, as a Jesuit, have violated Father Acquaviva's mandate that no Jesuit should justify tyrannicide, I would reply that I am merely suggesting that if the Church seeks to justify the killing of human beings in even a defensive war in the name of the people of a nation-state, the rights of those people against other forms of tyranny must also logically be defended. This is not a defense of tyrannicide but only a plea for consistency.

The Church and Wars of Revolution

Catholic theologians, at least until the 18th century, assessed the morality of revolutions in the same way that they evaluated other wars. It appears therefore that Aquinas, Suarez, and Bellarmine did not question the potential morality of a war of revolution. It can be argued, in fact, that the sentiments about revolution contained in America's Declaration of Independence are the product of Christian thinking or at least not inconsistent with that thought. That Declaration regarded it as self-evident that

> ... whenever any form of government becomes destructive of these ends [the securing of the unalienable rights of life, liberty, and the pursuit of happiness] it is the right of the people to alter or to abolish it, ...

Catholic thinking since at least the time of the French Revolution has, however, been sparse and negative on revolution. In 1832 Gregory XVI in *Mirari vos* spoke out against rebellion and sedition. Pius IX and Leo XIII are not known for any encouraging statements about resistance to entrenched power.

Vatican II avoided the subject completely. About the only source in modern times where the Holy See has even conceded the moral acceptance of revolution is paragraph 31 of Pope Paul VI's *Populorum Progressio.* The sanctioning of revolution is done only indirectly in the parenthetical phrase in the following:

> We know, however, that a revolutionary uprising—*save where there is manifest, long-standing tyranny which would do great damage to fundamental personal rights and dangerous harm to the common good of the country*—produces new injustices, throws more elements out of balance, and brings on new disasters. A real evil should not be fought against at the cost of great misery (emphasis added).

The three conditions which Pope Paul sets forth as justifying a "revolutionary uprising" would not be too difficult to verify in any number of underdeveloped nations where unrepresentative governments fail to provide for their people the "fundamental personal rights" of a decent standard of living and a reasonable opportunity to escape illiteracy. It is not surprising, then, that revolutionary uprisings are increasing in the Third World. In 1958 there were thirty-four violent revolutions. In 1965 the number rose to fifty-eight.

In the thirty-eight very poor countries of the world, with a per capita income of ninety dollars per year, thirty-two of these nations averaged in the years 1958 to 1965 almost two serious outbursts of extensive violence per year. During the same period the twenty-seven richest nations of the earth—countries which possess 75 percent of the earth's wealth but only 25 percent of the world's population—had only one important internal rising in all of the twenty-seven lands.[5]

Vatican II mentioned wars of revolution in only one place. It noted that "the complexity of the modern world and the intricacy of international relations allow guerrilla warfare to be drawn out by new methods of deceit and subversion. ... [and that] the use of terrorism is regarded as a new way to wage war."

The Church's theoretical stance on wars of revolution, therefore, can hardly be said to be very detailed. Pope Paul VI, moreover, in his trip to Latin America, was careful to urge the reform of social institutions only by peaceful means or within the existing framework. The bishops of the Third World generally endorse such a view.

World realities, however, suggest that the wars of the immediate future will be either thermonuclear wars between the great powers (which, according to Vatican II, are always immoral), or revolutionary guerrilla wars (which the Church has categorized as "offensive" and hence anathematized). Hence the Church has, in effect, declared as immoral any of the types of war which are likely to occur within the foreseeable future.

Pacifists—and even nonpacifists—would not object to such a judgment if the reasoning which led to it were put on display by the Church for the world to inspect. The tragic fact is that in most of the underdeveloped countries the only effective way to bring about a modicum of social justice is by revolution. This is probably more true in Latin America than in any other continent. Consequently the Church has left the one-third of its members who live in South America without any guidelines for a just revolutionary war. If for no other reason, the twenty-two hundred bishops of the world, and representatives of all religious groups, should come together in another ecumenical council to make some hard decisions about the morality of wars of revolution.

Notes

1. II *Sent.,* Ch. 44, Qu, 2, a, 2..

2. *The Catholic Encyclopedia,* vol. XV, p. 108.

3. *The New Catholic Encyclopedia,*vol. 14, p. 354.

4. *The Catholic Encyclopedia, ibid.,* p. 109.

5. H. Goss-Mayr, "Peace through Revolution," *Concilium,* 35, pp. 160-161.

7.

American Protestants and the Morality of War

THE PRESENCE within the Catholic tradition of an officially approved just war theory has without doubt inhibited Catholics from the initiatives for peace which have flourished in such an inspiring way among Protestants. Theoretically, there is no doctrinal difference on the theological level between Catholics and Protestants on what constitutes a just war. But the existence within Protestantism of the Quakers and such organizations as the pacifist Fellowship of Reconciliation has tended to give (or at least seem to give) the appearance of a much greater thrust against war in any form among Protestants than among Catholics. The conflict in Vietnam brought out this contrast more sharply than any previous war in American history. In fact the antiwar voices and forces in American Protestantism may well have had an enormous influence on Catholics, and have prompted countless numbers to reexamine and perhaps reject the just war theory.

The most difficult factor in assessing the attitude of Protestants in America towards the war is the presence throughout most of American history of an informal alliance of Protestant thought with America's domestic and foreign policy. America's attitudes to war have therefore inevitably been a reflection (or a distortion) of Protestant thought on this question. The excellent study by Robert W. Tucker, *The Just War—A Study in Contemporary American Doctrine,** provides an excellent evaluation of what Americans have thought and now think about the morality of war. Mr. Tucker does not attempt to identify the elements of America's conventional attitudes on war which derive from Protestant Christianity. Perhaps such a task is not really possible. But Mr. Tucker does delineate in a brilliant manner the inconsistencies and hypocrisies in the viewpoint of a nation which, partially because it has never been required to wage a war of actual aggression, generally retains the belief that it has on all occasions waged a purely defensive war against a wicked aggressor.

One of the many reasons why millions of Americans have opposed the war in Vietnam is that it does not fit into their concept of all previous wars in which Americans appear as peace-loving but reluctant heroes fighting against a monstrous force which maliciously seeks to destroy our way of life.

Protestant thought on war in American history has divided itself into the three traditional categories—the crusade, the just war, and the pacifist. It must be said, however, that Protestants in America have fallen into the crusade concept of war on almost every occasion when their government has declared war. One can speculate that if Protestants had retained within their tradition more of the natural law and its concept of the just war, they might have been less prone to adopt the extremes of either the crusade or the pacifist approach to war. But the speculation is of no value now since,

*Baltimore: Johns Hopkins Press, 1960.

due to the nature of modern war, the just war theory is as unsatisfactory in its results as either the crusade or the pacifist approach.

The just war theory of Augustine was accepted by Luther although he vigorously rejected the crusading concept of war.[1] But Luther's radical separation of the Kingdom of Christ from the Kingdom of the World would theoretically place warfare outside of the Church's affairs and squarely within the jurisdiction of the state, an entity whose existence, in Luther's thought, goes back to the order of creation and not of redemption. Logically this sharp demarcation would tend to lead to two moralities, with the state acting only to prevent a general anarchy of revenge to which fallen men are prone.

Luther, however, could hardly avoid pronouncing some judgment regarding the morality of all the dynastic, national, and religious wars of his age. He rejected the crusade not merely because it had been identified with the Church of Rome, but because it did not fit into his idea of the Church as radically separated from the government. But Luther condemned the uprising of the peasants as impossible to reconcile with the just war theory. For Luther, only the magistrate on whom God has bestowed the power to govern could use the sword.

In later life Luther conceded with the greatest reluctance that it might be permissible to rise up against an emperor who tried to eradicate the Protestant faith and compel Lutherans to go to Mass. But even here he suggested that the matter was political and that Christians should follow the judgment of the civic authorities.

Luther's dichotomy between the state and the Church has reappeared in a modified way in this century in the approaches to war of Karl Barth and Reinhold Niebuhr. The ultimate question involved would seem to be the extent of the redeemability of fallen human nature. If one feels that the state is created by men only as a coercive force to prevent violence and not as a natural concomitant of human nature, it follows that the wars waged by such a state are practically inevitable and that the Church therefore has no right or reason to condemn them.

Such an approach may result in a viewpoint which appears to be similar to that of Machiavelli who said this about war:

> When it is question of the safety of the country, no account should be taken of what is just or unjust, merciful or cruel, laudable or shameful, but without regard to anything else, that course is to be unswervingly pursued which shall save the life and maintain the liberty of the [fatherland].[2]

It is not, however, correct to charge, as some have, that Luther's radical dualism led inevitably to an implicit release of the temporal order from the scrutiny of moral norms. At most, one can say that Luther did not incorporate into his thinking on war all of the conceptual framework of Augustine; hence he does not have an integrated and consistent viewpoint on the role of the Church with regard to warmaking by the state.

Luther's followers appear to have exploited his ambiguities concerning the morality of war. In 1550 the Lutherans of Magdeburg developed a concept of armed resistance which justified the substitution by force of a form of constitutional government for a feudal rule. The advocates of this view adhered to the traditional notion that only a magistrate could use armed force on behalf of the common good. But in the absence at that time of the nation-state, lower magistrates were granted the power to use force even if their purpose was to restrain the conduct of higher magistrates. Through this device—and many others—Lutheranism was established by the state, although this was contrary to the basic inner logic of Luther's radical separation of the kingdoms of God and Caesar. It is this perpetuation of the union of altar and

throne which, more than any other factor, muted the prophetic witness which Christian churches might otherwise
have given against the militarization of the state.

Although there does not appear to be any truly theological
concept regarding war in Zwinglianism and Calvinism sig-
nificantly different from Lutheranism, the followers of John
Calvin, acting as a militant minority in France, the Nether-
lands, Scotland, and America, utilized the concept of war as
a crusade in frightening ways. These Calvinists turned away
from Luther's idea of the coercive function of the state as a
sad necessity and attributed to the civil government the duty
to support the true religion. War was thus looked upon as the
struggle of a religious society fighting in the name of the Lord
God of Hosts. Calvin's often repeated dictum that no consideration should be paid to humanity when the honor of God
is at stake once again appears to have the same result as the
approach of Machiavelli.

The story of how the reformers' theories on war were received and extended in England is long, complex, and
bloody. Preachers in that era, who sought to justify military
activities like those of Oliver Cromwell, obtained the texts
for their crusading sermons from Old Testament verses such
as Psalm 139: 21 which states: "Do I not hate them, O Lord,
that hate Thee?" Indeed as one reads of the fanaticism and
brutality of the post-Reformation period in England and the
era of the Thirty Years' War on the Continent, one can hardly
believe that all of the actors involved adhered to a religion
founded by a man whose central teaching could be epito-
mized in his own words: "But I say unto you, love your enemies" (Matt. 5: 44).

The aptitude of Christian leaders in Europe to justify a war
on the crusade principle was probably never more clearly
manifested than in the wars waged by the American colonies
against the aborigines. Roland H. Bainton, in his balanced
book, *Christian Attitudes Toward War and Peace,* asserts

that the New Englanders, in appealing to Moses to justify their extermination of the Indians, "reversed all previous Christian exegesis." He points out that "by common consent the conquest of Canaan had been ... a just aggressive war ... only because commanded by God."[3] In the absence of any further such mandate from God, the theocratic commonwealth presumably regarded itself as commissioned to subdue the Indians as if they were Amalekites. This at least is how Cotton Mather expressed the crusade he urged against the "Amalek annoying this Israel in the Wilderness."

In the 18th century the war against the Indians became a double crusade because the Indians were linked to the agents of the anti-Christ—the French missionaries and the papists. Bainton summed up the crusading wars of the colonies against the Indians by stating that the only word "to be written over the dealings of the white man with the red man is 'ruthlessness.'"[4]

This same "ruthlessness" has been the central characteristic of Americans in every war they have waged. It is dreadful to contemplate the fact that such "ruthlessness" is not only justified by appeal to Christian teaching, but that such teaching has been construed as actually compelling those who believe in it to wage war against their "enemies." The "holy war" concept so readily available to American Protestant churchmen is, of course, not their invention. It was one of the least defensible customs or usages of the Catholic Church which American Protestants were unwilling to reject.

The softening of the general Protestant viewpoint on war came about in America to some extent by reason of the mellowing of the rigors of Calvinism. In the 19th century the voices of persons such as William Ellery Channing and Ralph Waldo Emerson tended to lay the foundations of the ever more important pacifist movement.

The Civil War divided the Churches in America in ways which even in 1970 have not been rectified. The Churches in the South supported the Confederacy, with the result that three of the great Protestant denominations—the Methodists, the Presbyterians, and the Baptists—were divided over the morality of the war and the role of the Churches in speaking for or against it.

With the exception of the increasingly influential Quakers, the Churches in America during the 19th century followed more or less the patterns of religious thought in Europe. In the Old World the Churches usually supported the war initiated by the temporal ruler of the country in which the Churches were situated. This was also the pattern of the Orthodox Church in Russia, which supported the Czar on almost every occasion. During this period about the only voice from all of Europe that reached the world was that of the pacifist Tolstoy, who announced his position in the following striking language:

> All over Russia, from the palace to the remotest village, the pastors of churches, calling themselves Christians, appeal to that God who has enjoined love to one's enemies—to the God of Love Himself—to help the work of the devil to further the slaughter of men ... The same thing is going on in Japan. ... Japanese theologians and religious teachers no less than the military ... do not remain behind the Europeans in the techniques of religious deceit and sacrilege, but distort the great Buddhistic teaching by not only permitting but justifying that murder which Buddha forbade.[4]

Despite the obvious logic and the compelling cogency of Tolstoy's appeal, all the Churches in Europe and America found little if any difficulty in supporting their own nations when World War I erupted. It is indeed shocking to find, for example, the bishop of London urging his constituents to enter the First World War against Germany in these words:

> Kill Germans—to kill them, not for the sake of killing, but to save the world, to kill the good as well as the bad, to kill the young men as well as the old, to kill those who have shewn

kindness to our wounded as well as those fiends who crucified
the Canadian Sergeant. ... As I have said a thousand times, I
look upon it as a war for purity; I look upon everyone who dies
in it as a martyr.[5]

Endorsements of the First World War from Christian cler-
gymen of all denominations in every nation involved in the
war can be reviewed in the three-volume definitive work by
Anson P. Stokes and Leo Pfeffer, *Church and State in the
United States.** The rhetoric of the clergy and the incredible
ease with which they accepted the arguments advanced by
America and other nations are sufficient to warn any observer
that virtually all Christian Churches have been unable or
unwilling to resist the appeal of a temporal ruler for the
allegiance of citizens to a war which, however it is conceptu-
alized, must be taken as an exception to the divine law that
no man may morally take the life of another human being.

Again, immediately after Pearl Harbor, practically no
Christian Church in America had any difficulty in supporting
World War II. This is another indication of the enormously
troublesome phenomenon of the Christian Churches' ready
acceptance of the crusade theory of war on behalf of temporal and political objectives as these are generally conceived
in a moment of high public emotion and passion.

In the early days of World War II the ecumenical Protestant weekly, *The Christian Century*, attempted to develop a
fourth position which would be different from the three traditional concepts of war included in the ideas of pacifism, the
crusade, or the just war theory. *The Christian Century* stated
repeatedly in its editorials that in the global struggle of World
War II it could find no meaning and no morality. The editors
could not endorse the war nor could they unequivocally condemn America's participation in it.

This position was attacked by many individuals including
Reinhold Niebuhr, who felt very strongly that a war against

*New York: Harper & Row, Publishers, 1964.

a totalitarian system could be morally justified. Similarly, Dr. John C. Bennett protested strongly against making soldiers regard themselves merely as victims of a common tragedy. To Dr. Bennett, as to many other Protestants, the Second World War could be justified as a struggle to bring about the possibility of justice and freedom for men everywhere.

It seems fair to say that any traditional justifications of war which Protestants had used in both world wars were virtually annihilated with the mass incinerations at Hiroshima and Nagasaki. If Catholics and Protestants had followed different traditions with respect to the justification of war prior to the dropping of the atomic bomb, the separate traditions disappeared on that day in 1945 when the atomic era was born.

At the beginning of this period Protestants and Catholics adopted a similar attitude toward world peace, just as the Democrats and Republicans adopted a bipartisan foreign policy during the late 1940's when the Truman Doctrine and the Marshall Plan were initiated. In both instances a great error may have been committed by the Churches and by the political parties. Both groups sought to minimize their differences in order to form a united front against what was deemed the common enemy—a communist power with atomic warheads.

Almost immediately after the Christian Churches in America and the two dominant political parties asserted or assumed that world communism must somehow be contained, it became almost impossible for persons holding a contrary view to be heard. For a churchman to denounce or even criticize the mounting militarism in the country was deemed by most persons to be the equivalent of aiding and abetting the enemies of the Christian Church. A political figure who questioned the possibility or even the advisability of containing the forces of communism by military means was immediately stigmatized as "soft on communism" and deemed to be unpatriotic and un-American.

During the first ten years of the atomic era Christian

theologians spoke out, at least in a general way, to denounce war. The World Council of Churches, for example, stated in Amsterdam in 1948 that "we are one in proclaiming to all mankind: War is contrary to the will of God." Similarly, Pope Pius XII, in ways which have not received proper recognition, pointed out time and time again in his Christmas messages and in other communications to the world the horrors of the war, assumed to be inevitable, for which the capitalist and communist nations were preparing.

At least a few Christian theologians sought to think the unthinkable and respond to the question of whether Christian nations must allow annihilation rather than violate the fundamental rules of morality by participating in a war which would bring about the deaths of millions of persons. John C. Ford, S.J., for example, wrote in 1957 that if the alternative to the immoral use of atomic weapons were subjugation to an atheist regime or the extinction of the human race, "the followers of Christ should abandon themselves to divine Providence rather than forsake these [Christian moral] imperatives."[7]

Similar statements were made by Father Francis Stratmann in 1956 in his volume, *War and Christianity Today.**
Also, the collection of essays entitled *Morals and Missiles* placed several distinguished English Catholics on record as opposed in principle to the fundamental policy pursued by Western Europe and by America of threatening the communist nations with extinction by military devices.

The majority Catholic opinion, however, was considerably different; E. I. Watkin probably described it accurately when he wrote: "I fear most Catholics are persuaded that the evil of worldwide subjection to communist governments is so great that the employment of *any* means indispensable for preventing it, even the worldwide slaughter and ruin of atomic warfare, is justifiable."

Mr. Watkin rejects this viewpoint and states that "those

*Westminster, Md.: The Newman Press.

who urge it agree, however unintentionally and unconsciously, with the Marxists that material force is more powerful, therefore in the last resort more real, than spiritual. . . ." He then goes on to raise the fundamental question which virtually all Catholics and Protestants have sought to avoid during the twenty-five years of the atomic era:

> May it not be that God is inviting us to meet and defeat the challenge of modern materialism and confident secularism in all its forms, not only Marxist, by a supreme act of faith in His omnipotence which renounces methods of warfare which conscience plainly condemns?

The ambivalence within the Catholic community with regard to the possibility of a just war in the atomic era was mirrored and duplicated in Protestant thought. In Protestant writings about war, however, there remained a persistent flow of impressive literature advocating pacifism in some form. Pacifism in the years of the nuclear age has seemed to move from the fringes of Protestantism into its mainstream. Roland H. Bainton, for example, after reviewing various Christian viewpoints through the centuries with regard to war, ends up with a fundamentally pacifist orientation and concludes that "life is a precious boon, but life is not to be had at any price."[11]

A different view, as mentioned earlier, is held by the distinguished Protestant theologian, Paul Ramsey. Dr. Ramsey is undoubtedly the most eloquent and brilliant defender within both the Catholic and Protestant communities of the traditional just war theory. His 554-page volume, *The Just War: Force and Political Responsibility,*[12] is without doubt the most comprehensive synthesis and application of the traditional Catholic and Protestant theory of a just war which has ever been published; it is an updating of his many books and articles concerning the morality of war which cannot be underestimated in any way. Dr. Ramsey's careful and critical analysis of virtually every Catholic and Protestant writer on the subject of war can only be described as a masterpiece which rejects all forms of sophistry and sentimentalism in its approach.

Dr. Ramsey argues eloquently that "force still has its just uses" and that the "recovery of the just war doctrine" is essential if there is to be any rational dialogue and moral decision making about the ethics of warfare. He concedes that he is almost alone among Christian moral theologians in seeking to adapt and apply the just war theory to the problems of the nuclear age. At the same time it is clear that he has raised the fundamental question: Which moral principles, if any, can form the basis of a rational dialogue between religious men in a pluralistic society with regard to the totally new issue of the massive destruction of humanity—a possibility which is now an option in the thermonuclear world?

Dr. Ramsey boldly challenges the statements of the National Council of Churches, the World Council of Churches, and the somewhat ambiguous statements of Pope John in *Pacem in Terris*. While it is easy to say that Dr. Ramsey has separated himself from the main current of Protestant thought it is, on the other hand, difficult to deny that he is the most rational, logical, and forceful spokesman for a point of view which has not been repudiated with equal rationality or cogency by his critics.

One of Ramsey's basic major premises is that it is a right, if not a duty, of a Christian and of a Christian nation to contain communism by all available moral means. He suggests that the quality of life under a communist regime, and the suppression of religious freedom which could be anticipated in a Marxist state, offer adequate reasons for Christians to use military means to prevent a communist take-over of a neutral or of a Christian nation.

Because of the strength of Dr. Ramsey's position, his Christian critics have been unable or unwilling to assert that this major premise is erroneous. Most Christian writing against the horrors of war in the modern world have been almost silent about the fundamental question of whether it is morally permissible to engage in even conventional warfare against persons who have a political or ideological philosophy different from the ideas of capitalism and democracy which have dominated Western culture. In view of the fact that Paul Ramsey's critics will not face up to this essential question, his justification of war to contain communism is appealing and persuasive.

If a person assumes that the invasion of a nation by a foreign power, or the take-over by forceful means of the government of a nation by a political group within a country, justifies the taking of life to preserve the status quo and the existing government, he would then be obliged in logic to accept many of the Ramsey premises and conclusions. If, on the other hand, a person feels that the day has come for Christians and all persons to state that the gaining of a political objective does not justify the extinction of a human life, then the basic conclusions of Dr. Ramsey's position will be unacceptable.

Regardless of the ultimate attitude which a person takes toward Paul Ramsey's position, there is no doubt that Ramsey is one of the most articulate and rational moral theologians among all contemporary Catholic and Protestant writers on this subject.

Notes

1. For a description of Luther's not always consistent viewpoints on war, *see* Roland H. Bainton, *Christian Attitudes Toward War and Peace* (Nashville, Tenn.: Abingdon Press, 1960), pp. 136-143.

2. *The Prince,* chap. XVII.

3. Bainton, *op. cit.,* p. 167.

4. *Ibid.,* p. 172.

5. *Ibid.,* p. 204.

6. *Ibid.,* p. 207.

7. "The Morality of Obliteration Bombing," *Theology Digest* (Winter 1957), p. 9.

8. In Charles S. Thompson, ed., *Morals and Missiles* (New York: Oxford University Press, 1960).

9. *Ibid.*

10. *Ibid.*

11. Bainton, *op. cit.*

12. (New York: Charles Scribner's Sons, 1969).

8.

Vatican III and War

LOOKING NOW to the future of Roman Catholic opinion, what options would be open to the twenty-two hundred bishops who, having received detailed analyses of modern war from subcommissions and scholars of international relations, would have to make pronouncements on the question of when, if ever, war is justified in the contemporary world?

The Council could straddle the basic issues as Vatican II did and, with an eloquent plea for a more effective international system of world government, accept the existing balance of nuclear strength as the least unsatisfactory way to prevent the domination of the globe by the world's strongest military powers. On the other hand Vatican III could—not entirely without reason—take the position that modern war and all that it entails is so fearful and complex that no general rules of morality would be helpful in the evaluation of the specific issues in the total existential situation involved in a particular armed conflict.

A third—and in my judgment the best—option for the Council to follow would be to ban all war on the grounds that no version of Christianity can possibly tolerate as morally acceptable that destruction of vast numbers of persons which is inevitable in modern war. Such a position need not be one of pure pacifism but could be grounded on the contention that the conditions for a just war can never be verified because of the very nature of modern war.

A more rigorous version of this third option could be the view of the strict pacifist or the absolutistic interpretation of the mandate, "Thou shalt not kill." The long-standing exceptions to this principle recognized by the Church would seem to preclude the Church's acceptance at this time of the pacifist approach. But the worldwide inclination to reexamine everything which the Church has taught or done through the centuries could perhaps lead to a total reappraisal of the Church's views on war. Indeed Vatican II itself urged this when it demanded that war be viewed with "an entirely new attitude."

The option which is being urged here was expressed magnificently in a written intervention made by the late Cardinal Joseph Ritter during the fourth session of Vatican II. In this intervention, which was seen (and rejected) only by the members of a conciliar subcommission, Cardinal Ritter asked that the very possession of the arms required for a total war be categorically condemned. The statement of Cardinal Ritter was published shortly after his death; because of its compelling importance it deserves to be cited at length:

> My dear brothers! The possession of those arms which actually constitute the "balance of terror," even those which are aimed exclusively at deterring an adversary, already involve the intention—conditional perhaps but effective—of using

those arms: for possession without any intention of use would deter no one, would effect nothing. From the very nature of these arms, their enormous quantity and distribution, it can be seen what kind and how great a destruction is already projected. How then are we able to condemn every intention of destroying cities and at the same time, at least in part, approve the balance of terror?

What therefore should be done?

First: It is impossible to be silent in this matter. We have already promised the world the result of our deliberation.

Second: We must genuinely deliberate in order to produce some result. But we must deliberate, we must debate, about actual situations and conditions. What must be said about the morality of possession of those arms which actually exist, which constitute the very problem of the balance of terror, and what do we believe about those weapons which are already prepared for use?

We must admit that the present situation involves some elements which are good in themselves. Nations have accumulated arms with a primary intention not of waging but of avoiding war; at the same time national leaders are examining various plans for eliminating arms; and finally, as long as international institutions are not able to guarantee peace satisfactorily, and mutual trust among nations is lacking, other means of defense must seem inadequate. Nevertheless, in my judgment, the possession of arms which we must now consider should be condemned as wrong because it already includes the intention of total war and apart from that intention constitutes its very danger.

I believe, therefore, that there should be an absolute condemnation of the possession of arms which involve the intention or the grave peril of total war. After a careful consideration of the concrete situation, I believe there should be a clear and distinct declaration that the moral law requires that all urgently and without delay collaborate in the elimination of the possession of such armaments, no matter how great the difficulties which are feared and must be overcome.

As is evident, I propose this almost unwillingly. I would

willingly listen to and consider contrary arguments. But the demands of sincerity urge that we struggle with reality. We have already said much about the renewal of the Church, about manifesting Christ more clearly to men, and rendering the witness of our faith. "Now is the acceptable time" as it seems to me, "now is the day of salvation." Setting other considerations aside, we must become "true preachers of the faith of things to be hoped for—unhesitatingly joining our profession of faith to a life springing from faith." [Constitution on the Church, n. 35].[1]

This eloquent statement of Cardinal Ritter's is a precis of this book. It is a reasoned position leading to the inescapable conclusion that the mere possession of nuclear arms by a growing number of nations is morally indefensible.

Let us explore the vast implications of this position as the best option for Vatican III to follow.

The Third Vatican Council would be required to take a clear position on the present acceptability and credibility of the Church's traditional norms on war. It is certain, of course, that these norms do not directly depend on revelation except insofar as they are an implementation of the divine mandate against killing. In addition, Christianity teaches us to forgive injuries, to love our enemies, and to suffer insults with meekness. One can justify war only by the absence of clear disapproval of it in the Gospels.

In view of the sternness and seeming absoluteness of the divine directive in the Ten Commandments not to kill, it is always surprising and sometimes startling to see the multitude of rationalizations, glosses, and modifications which Christian theologians have affixed through the centuries to the unqualified words, "Thou shalt not kill."

St. Augustine was the first such theologian. He consistently refused to condone the taking of human life and "even denied to the individual the right to act in defense of his own life because such action might bring about the death of the aggressor."[2] Nonetheless Augustine made an exception to his general prohibition of taking human life when a person acted in a public capacity. He did this negatively, however, in that he exculpated the soldier from any personal sin if the soldier was killing an enemy in a just war.

A further inconsistency is latent in Augustine's position. Despite the fact that he would deny the right of a private individual to defend his person against a thief or a murderer, he would permit "the slaying of innocent civilians among the enemy population if the necessities of just war demand it."[3]

As has been noted, Vatican II has decisively rejected Augustine's acquiescence in the destruction of innocent civilian noncombatants. But Vatican II reaffirmed the basic exception to "Thou shalt not kill"—the just war—which was articulated and defended for the first time in Christian history by Augustine.

Would it be possible for Vatican III to reiterate the rejection of Augustine's view that noncombatants may be killed if this is necessary, and still accept his allowance of some wars as "just"? The answer would seem to be clearly No, since modern war, as never before, is total war. It is unrealistic and indeed almost foolish to use the term "war" today with any thought that a war fought in the 1970's could be less than total or, in other words, a conflict which did not inevitably involve the killing of civilian noncombatants. Clearly, the Israeli-Arab conflict cannot be restricted to its military participants. Nor could the Nigeria-Biafra civil war before its cessation in January 1970.

Vatican II tried to avoid confronting the inescapable reality that war today cannot be thought of in the way in which Augustine conceived it. The painful fact is that all modern war, however it may be confined or defined, becomes genocidal and consequently ends in the annihilation of noncombatants—a result which violates what Augustine might have allowed but which Vatican II declared to be absolutely immoral.

There are, of course, other reasons why Augustine's ideas on war should be set aside as obsolete and perhaps even contrary to that fuller understanding of Christianity which mankind, aided by grace, has developed through the centuries. One circumstance is the fact that Augustine was writing against the background of the Roman Empire which was at that time seeking a rationale by which to justify its warlike tactics to keep the "barbarians" outside the gates of "Christendom." As one reads Augustine, and as one studies Catholic statements today defending the American position in Vietnam, one cannot help but wonder about the extent to which Catholics in every century have elaborated a theory of a just war in a context where the war to be justified is designed, consciously or otherwise, to protect the status quo of a Christianized society against the invasions of "pagans" or "Communists."

The rhetoric and the reasoning of Pope Leo XIII's encyclicals on Church and State were analyzed by Father John Courtney Murray and shown to be documents written in the context of the Church in 19th century Europe fighting for its survival against countries which were more and more secularistic and nationalistic. In the light of the purposes of Leo XIII's encyclicals, Father Murray was able to demonstrate that these principles were not necessarily enduring but were rather a polemic suitable for the particular age in which Leo XIII wrote them.

A similar study could and should be done on the content and context of Augustine' theories on war. It might well demonstrate that Augustine (like Aquinas, Suarez, and other theologians after Augustine) did not enunciate abiding or permanent principles on the morality of war but, rather, doctrines applicable only to the existential reality of his own day.

We must always remember that in moral matters where

reason, guided perhaps indirectly by revelation, has been the source of moral principles, Christian men have throughout history made the most serious mistakes. For example, theologians condoned rather than condemned slavery, although today all moral thinking, including Catholic thought everywhere, would condemn the apartheid of South Africa—an institution which, however horrible, is a good deal less than slavery.

Another more contemporary and more dramatic example of error is the statement by Pius XII in 1957 that Catholics could not be conscientious objectors to participation in a particular war in which their nation was engaged.[4] Vatican II, followed by the American bishops in November 1968, urged, of course, that "it seems right that laws make humane provisions for the case of those who for reasons of conscience refuse to bear arms, provided, however, that they accept some other form of service to the human community."

One of the prime tasks of Vatican III would be, therefore, to assess the Augustine-Thomistic doctrine on war in its historical setting and to do so with a full recognition that through the centuries the most religious men have originated and followed moral theories thought to be based on reason and the natural law but which are in fact inconsistent with Christian truth. With this viewpoint Vatican III would have to recognize that the most serious inadequacy of Vatican II's statement on war is its failure to identify or evaluate the nature of the "goods," the preservation of which can justify the taking of life.

One of the principal goods deemed to justify a war in modern times is the right of a nation to self-determination. To exalt this right to such a lofty position is, of course, a very new development in legal or ethical thinking. The all too sparse literature written by Christians on the morality of war seldom if ever mentions the fact that Christ lived in a nation occupied by a foreign power—the Romans—but that presumably Christ and his compatriots were able to live in their fatherland without being forced to compromise their moral principles. It is true that the Jews of Christ's time offered considerable and constant passive resistance and civil disobedience to the Roman officials who governed and taxed them. But there is nothing in the words of Christ, the Gospels, or the Epistles of St. Paul to suggest that the Jewish people could have, in order to obtain the right of national self-determination, waged a "just" war against the Romans. Indeed the thrust of the New Testament, and especially of the Pauline Epistles, is to minimize the importance of a nation's right to self-determination by urging almost insistently that followers of Christ should obey their temporal rulers except in those presumably very rare instances where it is one's duty to obey God rather than men. This historical background of the age of Jesus and his apostles suggests at the very least that the right of a nation to self-determination has no basis in the New Testament. It may be that the silence about such a right in Scripture suggests that the reasoning which seeks to justify the death of human beings in the name of the right of national self-determination is based on an erroneous assessment of the relative value of each person's right to life vis-a-vis a nation's right to determine its own method of governing itself.

The collective belief of Americans in the adage "Give me liberty or give me death" is so inbred that it undoubtedly has had a profound influence on modern European history. Reflecting its own history, America has so exalted the right of national self-determination that the concept has found ready acceptance among other nations of the world. The American Revolution has come to represent for all mankind the prototype of an unquestionably moral "war of liberation." Even the most ardent Catholic educator in America would find it unthinkable to try to apply the traditional rules of a "just war" to the American Revolution. The rhetoric about "taxation without representation" and similar alleged tyrannies has, for Catholics and Americans, blotted out the fact that thousands of human lives were extinguished for the sole purpose of permitting Americans to have more to say about the way in which their political system would operate.

The idea is absolutely pervasive and unchallenged in modern society that war is justified if a nation is denied the right to have the exclusive power to select is own political institutions. Vatican II did not openly challenge this idea, and at least in an ambiguous way, approved of the concept by conceding that in the absence of a "sufficiently powerful authority at the international level, governments cannot be denied the right to legitimate defense. . . ." Does the Council mean that a government can shoot and kill nonviolent invaders from another nation who are seeking to take over the property and the political machinery of the occupied nation? When, in other words, can the "right to legitimate defense" be exercised by actions which take the lives of men?

Vatican II is unclear on this crucial issue and consequently gives us little light on the morality of allowing nations to extinguish human lives in order to protect a nation's property or its right to political self-determination.

Vatican III would be required to come to hard judgments about the fundamental question of whether any man or any nation can destroy human life in order to protect property or political goods. The Christian pacifist answers this question clearly and unequivocally by stating that no one can terminate the life bestowed on a man by God just to preserve some right to property or to a political system. Perhaps all Christians should answer the question the same way. But Christians—and Vatican II—qualify the divinely revealed ban on killing by extending what Vatican II called a nation's "right to legitimate defense" beyond the basic right to protect one's very existence into an ambiguous right to preserve the *quality* of existence which a nation has attained. The failure of

Vatican II to be clear and decisive on this issue is the compelling reason why Vatican III should be convened.

The reluctance of Christians to restrict the right of nations to kill only if they themselves would otherwise be killed has led to all types of fundamentally indefensible treaties in which the United States and many other nations are involved. These treaties openly justify and call for the killing of human beings to protect goods which are less precious than human existence itself.

The United States has, for example, entered into agreements under NATO, SEATO, and similar pacts to go to war to preserve the "territorial integrity" of some sixty nations of the earth. No American nonpacifist Christian has, to my knowledge, questioned the basic morality of America's committing itself to kill men in a war in order to prevent these men from trespassing on the land of a nation which is not their own. The treaties or commitments entered into by the United States over the past twenty years—like the SEATO agreement which (perhaps) led the United States into the Vietnam war—require in the ultimate analysis that America go to war, if requested, to expel trespassers from the land of a signatory nation even if the trespassing nation has not fired a shot or even taken over the government of the invaded nation. The treaties which implement America's foreign policy of containment are based, in other words, on the premise that a trespass on the territorial integrity of one nation justifies that nation and its allies in killing the trespassers.

Although no one seems to question the morality of one nation expelling by force (lethal if necessary) an intruder from its soil, no one presumably would assert a comparable right for the occupants of a neighborhood or for the members of a family. Even on the assumption that in a particular situation no civil or criminal law could adequately deal with such an intruder, would anyone suggest that in the absence of a

legal remedy a group of neighbors or the members of the
family could use force (of a deadly nature if necessary) to
protect their "territorial integrity"?

It may be, of course, that no nation violates the territorial
integrity of another unless the aggressor nation desires to
control the economic or political life of the invaded territory.
But even if the invading nation deprives the conquered people of the right to hold or to manage their own property and
the right to govern themselves, these rights still do not rise
to the level of the fundamental right to life itself.

Vatican II could have declared that the killing of men in
a war waged to defend property or to secure or preserve
political self-determination is immoral. It did not do so. And
for that reason I maintain that another ecumenical Council
should be convoked and should declare that there is no justifiable exception to God's command not to kill when the
protection of property or political self-determination are the
only reasons advanced to justify the killings.

Some persons will undoubtedly state that the Church cannot realistically deny to sovereign nations the right to use
deadly force to protect their territory and their political independence. These same persons would no doubt claim that it
is utopian to tell the insurgent and revolutionary nations of
the earth that they cannot kill men to vindicate their rights
to be free of colonial or other oppression.

Indeed, one noted Catholic expert on international law,
Professor William V. O'Brien, argued in an essay in 1960 that
continued insistence on the principle of the inviolability of
noncombatants in war might be "neither practical nor even
just."[5] This principle, ranked by all international scholars
prior to the age of nuclear war as immutable and unchal-
lengeable, may, according to Professor O'Brien, have become a victim of total war and hence obsolete in practice.

These critics of a more stringent morality with respect to
the moral permissibility of taking human life to attain a tem-

poral objective may well be able to quote moralists and Church documents from Augustine to Vatican II. At the same time these critics cannot fail to see a worldwide moral revulsion from every form of killing done in the name of some temporal or political objective. Hopefully this universal revulsion is a manifestation of the Holy Spirit breathing upon men everywhere and reminding them that it is God, and not man, who alone has the sovereign power over the life and death of every human being. Hopefully, also, a new ecumenical Council, called by the Church of Rome but participated in by all Christians and by nonbelievers from every nation of the earth, would articulate that message of the Holy Spirit and declare solemnly that no nation may extinguish a human life for any temporal or political objective.

Notes

1. *The St. Louis Review,* June 23, 1967. Cardinal Ritter's statement was also published in the *Catholic Worker* (July-August 1967), and is commented on at some length in James W. Douglass, *The Non-Violent Cross: A Theology of Revolution and Peace* (New York: The Macmillan Company, 1968).

2. Richard Shelly Haritgan, "Noncombatant Immunity: Reflections on Its Origin and Present Status," *Review of Politics* 29 (April 1967), pp. 204, 208.

3. *Ibid.,* p. 209. For an exposition and critique of Augustine's theory of war, *see* the same author's article, "St. Augustine on War and Killing: The Problem of the Innocent," *Journal of the History of Ideas* 27 (April-June 1966), pp. 195-204.

4. *See* citation in article on war in *The New Catholic Encyclopedia*, vol. 14, p. 804.

5. In William J. Nagle, ed., *Morality and Modern Warfare* (Baltimore: Helicon Press, Inc., 1960).

9.

Judaism and the Morality of War

ALTHOUGH THE OVERALL IMPRESSION of anyone familiar with the Scriptures could easily be an image of the Jewish people as a group devoted to war as a prime element of their policy, the fact is that throughout the Old Testament there are constant appeals to a vision and a dream of peace. The most famous of these appeals is contained in the famous words and the sublime vision of Isaiah wherein he envisages the ideal of universal peace in a society which will see "swords beaten into ploughshares and spears into pruning hooks."

All too little emphasis has been placed upon the great contribution of Israel and of its faith, Judaism, to the ideal of world peace. It is extraordinary that, in an age when war was the standard state of affairs, the prophecies of Amos and Micah urged everyone not merely to love peace but to *pursue peace*. The prophet Jeremiah is the classic example in Old

Testament times of the advocate of peace who was denounced by his own society but who was glorified by subsequent generations. Jeremiah, even when the armies of Babylon were hammering at the very gates of Jerusalem, vigorously and persistently opposed the taking up of arms on the part of king and countrymen against the enemy. Standing almost alone against the establishment of his day, Jeremiah appears to have denounced even defensive resistance and to have urged his people to submit rather than to be destroyed. Jeremiah, regarded as a traitor by his peers, was imprisoned and almost executed. It seems significant, however, that his bitter denunciation of his nation's policies was subsequently included within the canon of the Hebrew Scripture, and this incorporation can consequently be taken as an indication that active opposition to war in a specific and concrete manner is an option for the followers of Judaism which is completely consistent with the theology of that faith.

Despite all the appeals for peace in the Old Testament, however, one must admit that the major theme which has entered into America's view of peace and war is the one claiming that a nation can, and sometimes must, defend itself in the name of its national honor and of God's righteousness. All Christian writing with regard to the concept of a just war harkens back to some extent to Old Testament examples where, according to those who believe in the inspiration of the Scriptures, God himself commanded his chosen people to pursue a devastating war in order to bring about a victory for the people of Israel.

All the themes of belligerence which are so prominent in the Old Testament have been muted since the radical change in the life style of the Jewish people brought about by the destruction of Jerusalem and the dispersion of the children of Abraham into the Diaspora. The writings of learned rabbis through the last several centuries have stressed a belief in the all-conquering power of love and have de-emphasized the concept of the God of vengeance which appears to be a prominent theme in the Old Testament. Although the Jews were not in a position during the Christian centuries in Western Europe to work out any theory of a just war, several Jewish writers nonetheless have commented on this subject. Maimonides, for example, the great medieval Jewish philosopher, would permit war only if the enemy had explicitly refused to accept the duties of the minimal moral law incumbent on all human beings.

The writings of Maimonides reflect the Book of Deuteronomy which, while distinguishing between "commanded" and "permitted" wars, develops rules of warfare such as "sparing all women and children, fruit trees, and water supplies." Maimonides in his *Treatise on Kings and Wars* is indeed very modern when he writes: "When siege is laid to a city for the purpose of capture, it may not be surrounded on four sides, but only on three, in order to give an opportunity for an escape to those who would flee to save their lives."

Again, Deuteronomy is reflected in these words of Maimonides, which admonished that in waging war against a city, "You have to besiege it a long time. You must not destroy its trees, wielding an axe against them. You may eat of them, but you must not cut them down." These sentiments are a far cry indeed from the contemporary practices in Vietnam of "search and destroy," or "defoliation of crops," and other modern versions of the "scorched earth" policy.

The whole thrust and ideology of Judaism are, of course, contrary to armed violence of all types. The indomitable faith of Judaism in the oneness of God and the all-inclusive unity of God's children clearly proscribes any form of warfare waged on behalf of any temporal objective. The prayer with which Jews each Sabbath reach the climax of their liturgy in the Song of Peace expresses the centuries-old passion for peace in these words which entreat God to

... grant us peace, Thy most precious gift, O Thou eternal source of peace, and enable Israel to be its messenger unto the peoples of this earth. Strengthen the bonds of friendship and fellowship among the inhabitants of all lands. Plant virtue in every soul and may the love of Thy name hallow every heart. Praised be thou, O Lord, our God, giver of peace.

The passion for peace which is at the heart of Judaism has seldom been more evident than in the words and deeds of the Jewish community in America against the war in Vietnam. Many reasons can be cited for the virtual unanimity in the Jewish community against America's war in South Vietnam; but regardless of what these reasons may be, it seems fair to deduce that the Jewish mentality with regard to the struggle in Vietnam is at least in part traceable to the centuries-old mandate of Judaism that its followers must "pursue" peace.

Not a few individuals have remarked on the apparent contradiction between the viewpoint of the Jewish community in America with respect to Vietnam and the attitude of that same community toward the six-day war which Israel waged against the Arabs in June 1967 and toward future wars which may be necessary to preserve the territorial integrity of Israel.

I would suggest that if any case can be made out for war in the modern world, it can be made on behalf of the twenty-two year old state of Israel. However, I still find it very difficult, to verify, even in this instance, all of the requirements of the theory of a just war so familiar in Catholic and Protestant tradition. Among other difficulties, the test of proportionality may be very difficult to satisfy; it would seem predictable, for example, that thousands and possibly close to ten million Arabs may have to be killed in a land or air war in the Middle East if Israel is to protect even the preannexation boundaries of May 1967.

The anguish in seeking to develop some type of a theory

of a just war has of course tormented all Israel's citizens, particularly its young people who must—male and female alike—serve in the military forces for at least two years.

This struggle is perceptively portrayed in the book, *Dawn*, by a wise Jewish author, Elie Wiesel.[1] The story relates the anguish of a young Jew who, having survived a Nazi concentration camp, is one of the extremists in Israel during the time when that country was struggling to be born. The young Jew has been told by his superior officers to execute a British official as a reprisal. Throughout the long night prior to the event scheduled at dawn, the young man's mind and conscience are tormented by having to choose between the traditional Jewish values of the sanctity of life and the apparently unavoidable exigency of his nation. The argument on behalf of the newborn nation is stated as follows:

> We have no other choice. For generations we have wanted to be better, more pure in heart than those who persecuted us. You've all seen the result: Hitler and the extermination camps of Germany. We've had enough of trying to be more just, more peace-loving than those who claim to speak in the name of those virtues. If ever it's a question of killing off Jews, everyone is silent—there are twenty centuries to prove it. The commandment, "Thou shalt not kill," was given from the summit of one of the mountains here in Palestine and we were the only ones to obey it. But that's all over now. We must become like everybody else.[2]

Although not a few Jews throughout the world are troubled by the thought that the people of Israel have decided that, in the blunt words of Elie Wiesel, "We must become like everybody else," there is nonetheless a great deal that can be said to justify the defensive, and even to some extent, an offensive war waged by Israel. Such justification would have its roots in the international eminent domain accomplished by the United Nations in 1948 by which the State of Israel was created as an entity within the family of nations. An argument employed to fortify the legality of the existence of Israel as a nation-state is that the in-gathering of exiles which has been achieved in Israel is more than the birth of a new nation, since it is the coming together of people who, despite separation over a period of several centuries, have the same ethnic and religious values and tradition. On this basis, therefore, the argument can be made that Israel has not merely the right as a nation to defend its borders but also the right, as a cultural and religious minority, to insist that any threatened destruction of Israel is nothing less than genocide.

For Christians and others, who have gradually come to the conclusion that no war in the modern world can be justified, the situation of Israel causes acute anguish. That anguish was never more deeply felt than in the few months following the six-day war in June 1967. During those months, and even today, many and, perhaps, most Jewish leaders feel that Christians deserted them during and after their struggle with the Arab armed forces. It may be that the disappointment of many Jewish people with the silence of Christians concerning the war is one of the most profound points of tension between Jews and Christians in America. It seems unlikely, furthermore, that this area of tension will diminish, since the military needs of Israel will continue and may increase at the same time that Christians in America appear to be moving more and more towards the position that no war in the modern world can be justified. The nature of the dilemma confronted by Christians and others can be dramatized by the text of a telegram which I and several other Catholic and Protestant spokesmen in the United States received on June 3, 1967. That telegram asked us to wire our endorsement of the following statement:

> As Christians committed to pursue peace and oppose evil, we cannot remain silent in the face of threats of Arab leaders to destroy the people of the State of Israel. We abhor and condemn such threats as a sin against God and humanity.

We therefore call on the administration firmly to maintain its commitment and safeguard the integrity of the State of Israel and to restore the Gulf of Aqaba, an international waterway, whose blockade President Johnson has called "illegal and potentially disastrous" to the cause of peace.

Many Christians like myself, struggling to reconcile the war in Vietnam with whatever moral principles Catholic or Protestant traditions had preserved, did not respond in June 1967 to the request of Jewish leaders to urge the United States government to live up to its commitments.

The six-page statement of the National Council of Churches, issued on July 7, 1967, created confusion and additional misunderstanding between Christians and Jews in America with regard to the support which Christians would give to the embattled State of Israel. At the end of the summer of 1967 Rabbi Balfour Brickner stated in the September 18 issue of *Christianity and Crisis* that most communities of Jews and Christians had, with respect to the issue of Israel, "passed each other like ships in the night, obscured for the most part by the fog of mutual misunderstanding."

The misunderstanding on the part of Christians stems, it seems to me, from the claim made by some—but apparently not all—Jews that Israel is, in essence, an integral part of Judaism; it is thereby entitled to protection not merely as a nation but as an entity to which the doctrine of total religious freedom emphasized by the Second Vatican Council should be applicable. This claim undoubtedly has been one of the many reasons why Christians in America, during the first twenty years of Israel's existence as a nation, have been silent on almost every occasion about the aggression and genocide which the Arab nations have threatened against Israel.

The centrality of Jerusalem and Israel to Judaism derives from the belief implicit in Judaism that the Messiah will in fact come to the Chosen People in the land of Israel. Consequently, Jerusalem means far more to Jews than Rome means to Catholics or Canterbury to Anglicans. Indeed certain Jewish intellectuals have developed what might be called a "theology of place" with respect to Israel.

In view of this profoundly held conviction on the part of many learned Jews, it is important to explore the implications of the negative attitude which the Vatican has had concerning the existence of Israel as a nation. Whatever little documentation exists with regard to the relationship between the Vatican and Israel is collected in a volume entitled *Three Popes and the Jews,* * by Pinchas E. Lapide. This book reveals an almost complete absence of thought about Israel in Vatican circles. For reasons which are very difficult to understand the Holy See has never extended diplomatic recognition and accreditation to Israel. It is not clear that Israel has lost any specific benefits by the absence of such liaison, but it seems evident that the cordial but cool attitude which the Holy See has adopted toward Israel is based on a desire on the part of Rome not to disturb its relations with Christians in Arab lands and to prevent misunderstandings with the leaders of those nations.

The neutral or negative stance of the Vatican towards Israel does not necessarily suggest any theological suppositions or any unconscious prejudices latent in Catholicism from which this attitude might consciously or otherwise proceed. On the other hand the newly constituted State of Israel may be predicated in part on a theology of Zionism which would so interlink Judaism and Zionism that the nation-state of Israel deserves very special and unique recogniition and protection by the Holy See and by the family of nations. With this in mind, is it fanciful to suggest and to urge that the Third Vatican Council meet, not in Rome but in Jerusalem? Clearly the Christians of the world—and perhaps particularly Catholics—owe a profound duty to the Jewish people to develop some kind of ethical system by which the family of nations

*New York: Hawthorn Books, Inc., 1967.

could arrive at a consensus regarding the morality of war—
unless, of course, organized humanity could abolish war
forever.

It is understandable why most spokesmen for Israel are
reluctant to treat that state as anything more than a nation
created as a political settlement by the United Nations acting
on behalf of anguished humanity which had witnessed the
extinction of six million Jews before and during the Second
World War. It seems to me, however, that if the Jewish community is of the opinion that Zionism and Judaism are linked
theologically and that Israel, as a result, is a unique type of
nationsynagogue, then the Jewish community must tell
Christians about their conviction that Zionism is an essential
flowering of Judaism; otherwise, any person who is anti-Zion-
ist may be mistakenly labeled as anti-Semitic also. Thus if war
breaks out in the Middle East, the present confusion in the
minds of virtually all Christians in America regarding the
interconnection between Judaism and Zionism will certainly
result in misunderstandings which will be even more serious
than the frustrations felt by both the Jewish and Christian
communities in America after the six-day war in June 1967.

While defenders of Israel in America are working dili-
gently to persuade Christians that a war in which Israel
would be engaged against Arab nations deserves their support, it is becoming distressingly clear that new leftist elements in the United States are escalating a campaign which
questions the fundamental right of Israel to its place in the
Middle East. It is difficult to assess the strength of this new
movement which utilizes the literature of the Organization of
Arab Students (OAS), a group with a membership of approximately one thousand which quite understandably seeks to
exploit those who have radical and revolutionary ideas with
regard to the Third World. When the rhetoric of these individuals is applied to the Middle East it results in a vigorous
advocacy of the restoration of Palestine as the Arab home-

land. It suggests that Arab nations in the Near East must engage in a prolonged military struggle against the Zionist-imperialist-reactionary forces which support Israel and that the recommended revolution should be similar to that launched by the progressive revolutionaries of China, Algeria, Cuba, and Vietnam.

A few radical black groups have announced support of the position of the OAS. One of these is the Student Non-Violent Coordinating Committee (SNCC), which apparently was won over by the analogy made by the OAS between "the Arabs in occupied Palestine and the black people in the American ghettos." Both groups, OAS has proclaimed, "must be liberated from exploitation, oppression, brutality, intimidation, and prejudice."

Al Fatah, the major Palestinian terrorist organization, sought through various instrumentalities in America to convince young radicals that the death of Che Guevara and the phasing-out of the Vietnam war should prompt them to turn their energies to a war of liberation for the Arabs against Israel, which they describe as the "tool of Western capitalist imperialism" to suppress the national liberation struggle of the Third World.

Anti-Israel sentiments are relatively common in the literature of the contemporary black radical movement. Anti-Semitism among some black persons has become anti-Israel by simple extension. Stokely Carmichael, an activist in the Black Panther party, spoke in 1969 to the OAS national convention at the University of Michigan. Mr. Carmichael pledged black militant armed support—to the death if necessary—for an Arab victory over Israel. He went on to state that "we will work closer with the Arab students wherever we can. Our eyes are now open; we have begun to see this trickery of Zionism; we have begun to see the evil of Zionism, and we will fight to wipe it out wherever it exists. . . ."

The Black Muslim religious sect has adopted a similiar pro-

Arab viewpoint. Black Muslim literature and rhetoric stress the religious affinity between the Arabs surrounding Israel and the Black Muslim revolutionaries in the United States.

Although it is difficult to make any generalizations regarding the future of revolutionary thought in America, it seems clear that many radical young Americans would greet any war that might break out in the Middle East between Israel and the surrounding Arab nations with attitudes which, up to this time, have not entered either the mainstream of American thought on Israel or any of the individual or collective viewpoints concerning the morality of war in the modern world.

To most Americans, the very thought of a possible land war in the Middle East is horrifying because, for one thing, the moral issues in such a war would be even more complex than those involved in the Vietnam struggle. Israel, in addition to being a Western-style democracy, is to some extent a theologically oriented nation-state almost entirely unprecedented in the history of Western culture. On the other hand the thirteen Arab nations, with a population of some seventy million people, also have a profound and rich culture going back through the centuries. Americans, who know all too little about either of these cultures, would be required in the event of a Middle East war to make some kind of moral assessment of the equities on each side. The mere contemplation of such an eventuality reveals once again the threadbare character of any test or norm by which Christians or others could judge the moral or ethical nature of a particular armed conflict.

As things stand now, the one certainty about any war in the Middle East is the inevitability of massive civilian casualties. Modern war means not the death of soldiers but the death of noncombatants. In the First World War only 5 percent of the casualties were civilians. In the Second World War 48 percent of the dead and wounded were civilians; and in the

Korean War, 84 percent. The Vietnam War brought civilian casualties to a new all-time high of 90 percent. In a war in the Middle East it could be predicted that the death and casualty rate among soldiers would be even less than the 10 percent rate in Vietnam; the possible or potential millions of civilian casualties staggers the mind and the imagination.

One of the essential points of conflict between Israel and the Arab nations centers on the explosive issue of the homeland. Arab spokesmen claim that they have been dispossessed of the land and homes which their fathers built and owned. The Israelis for their part claim that the land surrounding the Jordan River belongs to them by a mandate of God himself by long tradition, and by the mandate of the family of nations speaking through the United Nations in 1948.

The tangled web of politics, nationalism, religion, and Russian infiltration in the Middle East would almost suggest that it is virtually impossible to arrive at any moral norm which could be applied to an outbreak of armed conflict in that troubled area. Yet America is committed to protect the territorial integrity of Israel and other Middle East nations in the event of an invasion by a foreign power, and there is a strong possibility that implementation of that commitment will be called for. But if the SEATO treaty has not been self-explanatory in connection with our obligations in Southeast Asia, then the treaties which the United States has signed with nations in the Middle East can hardly be expected to be clear or unequivocal.

The complexity of the situation, with all its frightening ramifications, dramatically points up the simplistic reasoning behind United States foreign policy—a policy predicated almost exclusively on the proposition that the United States should do all in its power to contain communism. It offers no answer to the question of what the United States should do regarding Arab nationalism, theologically-oriented Zionism, or the revolutionary aspirations of Moslem insurgents. Perhaps its ultimate irrationality is the almost exclusive emphasis placed on the right of political self-determination of the nations in that area of the world. In short, America's goal—with which it seems almost obsessed—has not been the elimination of hunger, disease, or illiteracy, but only the preservation by all military means necessary of the political self-determination of both Israel and the Arab nations.

Nor does American policy inquire whether any nation in that part of the world can long preserve its political autonomy if its people are deprived of those goods and benefits which are generally enjoyed by citizens of both communist and capitalistic countries. By what set of moral principles did the United States come to the determination that its role in the world is to preserve the political status quo, even though at least one-half of the world's people suffer from malnutrition and lack of education?

Obviously, America's foreign policy must be drastically revised, particularly when we consider the fact that since 1946 the United States has spent approximately $950 billion on the arms race. However understandable this policy may be in the light of the traditional policy of securing the peace by preparing for war, there is nevertheless abundant evidence that, by becoming the greatest merchant of arms in the history of mankind, the United States has made war almost inevitable.

There must surely be some moral principles implicit in religion and rationality which can be utilized and developed to bring about a more satisfactory redistribution of the wealth of the world and, consequently, a greater hope in the long run for world peace.

It is to these principles that we now turn with the hope that some spiritual norms can emerge by which humanity may dismantle what the Second Vatican Council has called the "altogether monstrous" equilibrium of terror which dominates the earth and devastates its resources.

We will also explore the misconceptions and illusions about communism and Marxism which have become a dangerous part of the American mind. Closely related to the near-hysteria over communism which affects Americans, particularly American Catholics, is the fear which all Americans have concerning world federalism—an idea whose realization is demanded by Catholic teaching and tradition.

Notes

1. (New York: Hill & Wang, Inc., 1961).
2. *Ibid.*

10.

Hunger, Poverty, and War

IN EVERY CONSIDERATION of the countless proposals through the centuries to eliminate war, one is haunted by the question whether it is realistic to expect mankind at any time to give up war as something totally unworthy of civilized mankind. One frail hope that mankind can reform in this direction is the voluntary abstention up to this time by most warring parties in the world from biological and chemical warfare.

The overall record of mankind, however, is not encouraging. In the book, *The Lessons of History*, by Will and Ariel Durant,[1] it is stated that "In the last 3,421 years of recorded history only 268 of these years have seen no war."[2] In view of such statistics one is tempted to feel that the numbers of wars like the numbers of thefts, lies, and acts of adultery, are constant and will remain so in human history. This pessimistic and even fatalistic view of mankind can be supported not only by history, but by some interpretations of the Catholic definition of original sin, and certainly by the Calvinist view of human nature which, at least until recently, has constituted a part of the American ethos.

The immense amount of literature concerning the history and causes of war in civilized society also indicates that the possibility of phasing out war is seemingly unachievable. I have been overwhelmed more than once by the mere inspection of the huge collection of books in any important library dealing with every aspect of war. Despite all this literature it is apparent that no one knows precisely the causes of war nor can anyone provide any reliable barometer for predicting when it will break out. Like domestic violence, war is a phenomenon on which historians, psychologists, sociologists, and theologians, singly and collectively, have shed very little light.

There is, moreover, no analogue of war in human history. All forms of personal immorality continue to recur at every moment in history and in all classes of individuals; but the perpetrators of these immoral acts never claim that the extinction of thousands of lives can be morally justified because such destruction is necessary for the attainment of some temporal or political objective. There seems to be, furthermore, some amelioration of private conduct since, for example, we no longer have such barbarities as trial by ordeal. In the area of warfare, however, each century seems to introduce new forms of barbarism. Warfare through the centuries has increased in ferociousness as it has grown from vendettas between tribes to wars between nations and now to armed conflict between all of Western Europe and the United States against at least one-third of humanity, or some 700,000,000 persons who live in Communist China, Russia, and the satellites.

In every century the generals and the rulers of nations smile benignly at the philosophers and moralists who rise up

and denounce war. Humanity at various times—and particularly at the present moment in history —has the profoundest
empathy with these philosophers and moralists who oppose
war, but at the same time mankind continues to glorify
Charles Martel who kept France and Spain from being Mo-
hammedan at the Battle of Tours in 732. In a more contemporary context it is most difficult and indeed almost impossible
to find, even among the most militant "doves," persons who
will repudiate the participation of America in the Second
World War as immoral. The generals who turned back a Hitler will be honored with gratitude by those whose political
boundaries and way of life have been preserved, regardless
of the destruction and destitution caused to the "enemy." In
view of mankind's veritable addiction to war it often seems
naive and unrealistic for philosophers and moralists even to
spend their intellectual energy and efforts on proposals to
limit their number and severity. But in this generation, almost
perhaps as never before, there is a compelling feeling which
Will and Ariel Durant express in these words: "There is
something greater than history. Somewhere, sometime, in the
name of humanity, we must challenge a thousand evil prece-
dents and thereto apply the Golden Rule to nations ... or at
least do what Augustus did when he bade Tiberius desist
from further invasion of Germany (A.D. 9)."[3]

The Durants state, in a moving paragraph that deserves
quotation in full, the cry which the Second Vatican Council
issued when it told us to think of war "with an entirely new
attitude." The Durants imagine an American president
speaking to the world and to the leaders of China and Russia
as follows:

> If we should follow the usual course of history we should make
> war upon you for fear of what you may do a generation hence.
> Or we should follow the dismal precedent of the Holy Alliance
> of 1815, and dedicate our wealth and our soundest youth to
> suppressing any revolt against the existing order anywhere.

But we are willing to try a new approach. We respect your peoples and your civilizations as among the most creative in history. We shall try to understand your feelings and your desire to develop your own institutions without fear of attack. We must not allow our mutual fears to lead us into war, for the unparalleled murderousness of our weapons and yours brings into the situation an element unfamiliar to history. We propose to send representatives to join with yours in a persistent conference for the adjustment of our differences, the cessation of hostilities and subversion, and the reduction of our armaments. Wherever, outside our borders, we may find ourselves competing with you for the allegiance of a people, we are willing to submit to a full and fair election of the population concerned. Let us open our doors to each other, and organize cultural exchanges that will promote mutual appreciation and understanding. We are not afraid that your economc system will displace ours, nor need you fear that ours will displace yours; we believe that each system will learn from the other and be able to live with it in cooperation and peace. Perhaps each of us, while maintaining adequate defenses, can arrange nonaggression and nonsubversion pacts with other states, and from these accords a world order may take form within which each nation will remain sovereign and unique, limited only by agreements freely signed. We ask you to join us in this defiance of history, this resolve to extend courtesy and civilization to the relations among states. We pledge our honor before all mankind to enter into this venture in full sincerity and trust. If we lose in the historic gamble, the results could not be worse than those that we may expect from a continuation of traditional policies. If you and we succeed, we shall merit a place for centuries to come in the grateful memory of mankind.[4]

Although this creative and imaginative proposal does not refer specifically to the need of eliminating poverty and disease before nations can coexist in peace, it assumes that this objective will be attained if the capitalist and communist economic systems are allowed to interact, to learn from each other, and to live together in peace. That interaction is not now possible, but the nations of the Free World should be persuaded that they must act more swiftly than ever before to lessen the oppression of poverty which is embittering those who daily suffer its scourge.

It is difficult to prove empirically that the presence of abject poverty or illiteracy is a necessary cause of war; nonetheless, one must grant that the poor nations simply will not tolerate the existence of great affluence in a world—which is their world, too—in which distances between nations have been virtually eliminated by radio and television. It is plainly this assumption which is at the heart of Pope Paul's remarkable encyclical, *On the Development of Nations.* Prior to this, a brilliant description of the idealism and the realism which should inspire the rich nations in this matter was expressed by President Kennedy in his inaugural address:

> To those peoples in the huts and villages of half the globe struggling to break the bonds of mass misery, we pledge our best efforts to help them help themselves, for whatever period is required—not because the communists may be doing it, not because we seek their votes, but because it is right. If a free society cannot help the many who are poor, it cannot save the few who are rich.

The substance of this pledge was first announced as an American commitment by President Harry S. Truman on January 20, 1949 at his inauguration. In his talk on this occasion Truman outlined four points that would guide his policy. Three of the points were immediately forgotten, but the fourth was seized by the public and the press, and achieved a status of its own as "Point Four."

Point Four called attention to the low living standard of the majority of the world's people and made a commitment that the technical knowledge which America possessed would be shared with the underdeveloped countries so that they could take advantage of the newly acquired skills of the industrialized world.

In President Truman's *Memoirs* he suggested an argument on behalf of such aid to the Third World partially on the basis of reparation or restitution. Commenting on the Point Four program he wrote:

> I knew from my study of American history that this country was developed by the investment of foreign capital by the British, the Dutch, the Germans, and the French. These countries invested immense sums in the development of our railroads, mines, oil lands, and the livestock industry. ... It seemed to me that if we could encourage stabilized governments in underdeveloped countries in Africa, South America, and Asia, we could encourage the use for the development of those areas of some of the capital which had accumulated in the United States.[5]

Unfortunately, the humanitarian objectives, set forth by Presidents Truman and Kennedy for giving assistance to poverty-stricken countries, have not diminished the disparity between the rich and the poor nations or decreased in any notable way the scale of world poverty and hunger. It may well be, however, that if the United States and the other affluent nations of the earth had in fact been faithful and extraordinarily generous to the commitment made in Point Four, the hundred or more nations, which are today suffering the agonies of decolonization, would be substantially more stable and a good deal less prone to war and revolution.

One of the many factors which decreased the effectiveness of foreign aid was its use—particularly after the presidential elections of 1952—as a weapon in the Cold War. Under the impact of the Korean War the Eisenhower administration sought to safeguard all the frontiers of the world against communist expansion. Consequently the White House, during the years 1953 to 1960, preferred to concentrate on giving military aid and economic support to those countries that were ready to show their commitment to the West by joining in a pact with the United States. The countries which chose to remain "neutral" or "nonaligned" were therefore offered much less help. An almost inevitable result of such a policy was the alliance of American with political regimes such as South Korea, Formosa, and South Vietnam—nations whose regimes in some instances needed a firm union with the United States in order to remain in power.

Soviet assistance to underdeveloped countries during this same period was on a much smaller scale, but was generally concentrated on politically sensitive and important countries rather than upon those nations which were allied to the Soviet Union. This type of arrangement allowed the Soviet Union to exploit the propaganda value in the fact that it did not attach "strings" to its aid. This policy of cultivating the nonaligned nations also gave Russia the advantage of acquiring friends among the neutral nations of the world while simultaneously avoiding the humiliation of being a poor second in offering aid to those nations to which the United States had made commitments.

If there is one point of agreement in the vast amount of literature dealing with various forms of foreign aid since the end of the Second World War, it is the common conviction that such aid should not be dispensed by any nation but rather by an international entity such as the World Bank. To repeat, aid in the past generation has obviously been utilized as a weapon in the Cold War. For this reason it is simply not possible to assess the extent to which further infusions of such aid on a massive basis, carried out by an international agency, would be able to promote at least enough stability within newly constituted nations to deter them from wars of aggression against their neighbors or from revolutionary wars against the regime in power. There is also the possibility, of course, that even an internationalized system of aid to underdeveloped nations may in some cases promote international tension, as was the case with American aid to Pakistan. This, however, seems a risk worth taking.

Whatever conclusion one might reach with respect to the

effectiveness of foreign aid over the past twenty years, one must concede that the two billion dollars offered by America in 1970 for this purpose is totally inadequate to prevent war, to stabilize nations, or to do anything significant with regard to the ever escalating disparity between the rich and the poor nations of the world.

The sum expended each year by the United States for nonmilitary foreign aid is so small a part of its gross national product that America is not even among the top ten nations with regard to the amount which annually it bestows on the less developed members of the family of nations.

No one is naive enough to pretend that if the United States, joined by all of the rich nations of the earth, were generous and heroic enough to foster a global Marshall Plan which would bring the poor nations up to a decent standard of living, that this would automatically decrease the likelihood and incidence of wars. It is indeed conceivable that some regimes would utilize the newfound affluence of the nation for military purposes based on personal ambitions, racism, or any one of the countless other motivations which have prompted kings, emperors, and rulers to bring their people into armed conflict with their neighbors. It is even conceivable that new nations, suddenly affluent, would waste all their assets by joining the very small group of nations now possessing the atomic or hydrogen bomb.

Clearly, therefore, the elimination of the disparity between the poor and rich nations is but a step to a new and unexplored world. But the perpetuation of the enormous disparity will almost inevitably lead to a series of intranation revolutions or to some type of international conflict.

That inevitability, however, is unlikely to offer sufficient motivation to the present generation of citizens and rulers in the affluent nations to share any significant part of their riches with the underdeveloped nations. In addition, rationalizations to support the sheer tokenism of foreign aid will be largely unnecessary, since the poor nations of Africa and Asia have scarcely a voice to be heard in confrontation with the massive economic, industrial, and military power of the capitalist and communist sectors of the world.

The only pragmatic motivation which Europeans and Americans have to develop a Marshall Plan for the Third World is the fear that if the West does not do it, Russia most certainly will. Even this eventuality, however, has not developed into a reality which will goad the noncommunist nations to lower, even slightly, their standards of living, in order to aid the hundreds of millions of black and yellow people who lead lives without food, without medicine, and without hope.

Perhaps the silent masses liberated from their colonial masters during the past twenty years could be compared to the Negroes in America prior to Martin Luther King, Jr. and the freedom movement which began in 1955. It is a truism that whatever betterment has come to America's black people during the past fifteen years has been due almost entirely to their militancy and to the vigor with which they have asserted their demands for equality and freedom. Can the peasants of Asia, the tribesmen of Africa, and the dispossessed of Latin America obtain a voice and a leader which will force the affluent nations to do for them what a guilt-stricken America has done for its black citizens? What would happen if Catholics actually believed and acted upon those stark Christian principles enunciated by Pope Paul in *The Development of Peoples,* where it is stated as an undeniable Christian principle that the rich man must share his abundance with the poor man? The Epistle of St. James contains words which seem appropriate to describe the attitude of American Christians concerning the continents of countless men and women who are ravished by hunger. St. James asks: "If a brother or sister be naked, if they lack their daily nourishment, and one of you says to them: 'Go in peace. Be warmed

and be filled,' without giving them what is necessary for the
body, what good does it do?"

St. Ambrose, cited by Pope Paul in the encyclical on the
development of nations, sums up the attitude of the early
Church fathers regarding the duties of those with superfluous
goods in these words:

> You are not making a gift of your possessions to the poor
> person. You are handing over to him what is his. For what has
> been given in common for the use of all, you have arrogated
> to yourself. The world is given to all, and not to the rich.

Pope Paul, reflecting the views of all of his predecessors,
declared that the same duty of sharing one's wealth which
exists for individuals exists also for nations. Very specifically
he states that "the rule which up to now held good for the
benefit of those nearest to us, must today be applied to all the
needy of this world." The same idea was concretized by the
pope in his Bombay address, in which he called for the establishment of a great world fund to serve all the peoples of the
earth who suffer from destitution and ignorance.

What complex set of reasons makes American Catholics
almost totally unaware of the bold and challenging moral
principles enunciated by Pope Paul in the encyclical, *On the
Development of Peoples,* issued on Easter Sunday in 1967?
Does he pinpoint the essential reason when he notes that
"avarice is the most evident form of moral underdevelop-
ment" in highly developed nations? Or is the reason more
directly related to the inherently self-centered nature of
capitalism which, as Pope Paul sees it, is a system "which
considers profit as the key motive for economic progress,
competition as the supreme law of economics, and private
ownership of the means of production as an absolute right
that has no limits and carries no corresponding social obligation"?

Whatever the reasons may be for the persistent and almost

incredible isolationism of American Catholics, it is clear that
the bishops have done virtually nothing to create in the
minds and hearts of their people any desire to take the initiative and to infuse into public officials a compelling conviction
about the duties of the most affluent nation in the history of
humanity towards the millions in the world who, in the words
of Pope Paul, "are still buried in wretchedness, and are the
victims of insecurity and the slaves of ignorance."

Pope Paul seems to acknowledge the failure of the hierarchies of the world when he says that "it belongs to the laymen, without waiting passively for orders and directives, to
take the initiative freely and to infuse a Christian spirit into
the mentality, customs, laws, and structure of the community
in which they live."

What would happen in America if a substantial number of
Catholics, reinforced by a number of non-Catholics, proposed and worked militantly for a United States foreign aid
program which would expend each year some fifty billion
dollars, or 5% of the gross national product in the year 1970?
Would not the endorsement by Catholics of such a plan be
a magnificent way of giving witness to the continued vitality
and validity of one of the crucial questions of the New Testament: "If someone who has the riches of this world sees his
brother in need and closes his heart to him, how does the love
of God abide in him?"

Perhaps Catholics might develop a theory of justice based
on reparation or restitution. Reparations are due the Third
World, the theory would elaborate, because the United
States, in pursuing for the past twenty years a fantastically
expensive military nonsolution to the social problems of the
underdeveloped nations, has in fact cheated those countries
of the nonmilitary aid which it had an obligation to give to
assist these countries to emerge from the ashes of colonialism.

If the rhetoric surrounding the whole question of "reparations" from the churches in America is so emotion-laden that

even the concept of reparations is deemed inappropriate for the international order, a plan for the poor nations could be developed along the lines of the "Freedom Budget." This is a document, signed by some of America's leading economists, recommending the expenditure of $160 billion over the next ten years to phase out poverty in every form in rural and urban America. The Freedom Budget or, as it is sometimes called, the Marshall Plan for the North, argues cogently and with documentation that the expenditure of $16 billion per year over a decade would recreate the ghettos of the country, phase out substandard schools, and create adequate housing for all of the 230 million Americans who will populate the country in 1980.

Similar reasoning could be used to develop a powerful line of argument that the annual expenditure by the United States government of $50 billion would prompt other affluent nations to spend comparable sums and would bring new waves of hope and self-confidence to millions of persons who would feel that for the first time they might be able to escape from those conditions which, in the words of Pope Paul, are "unworthy of the human person."

It is significant that the reaction of most Americans to the idea of paying reparations to the blacks is the same as their reaction to any proposal for massive aid to underdeveloped nations. Almost immediately most say that such payments would be "wasted" or spent for the selfish purposes of those who are the first recipients of such funds. The opponents of any additional aid to the underdeveloped countries employ rhetoric which portrays such aid as "going down rat holes" or into the pockets of corrupt dictators who have seized power by a military coup. With few exceptions, Americans will not concede that massive aid is imperative and that consequently *some way* must be found to distribute it in a just and efficient way.

The middle class in America has been sardonically described as deeming themselves to be the "final solution." But it would be underestimating the power of the Holy Spirit and exaggerating the inherent selfishness of men not to hope and indeed to expect that from the "silent majority" of Americans there would emerge a new group who would agree with Pope Paul that the modern word for peace is development.

Even if the teachings of the Second Vatican Council on atomic war are inadequate, and even if the concept of a just war as transmitted in Catholic tradition no longer seems relevant, Catholics can be grateful and proud that the Holy See has, as almost no other institution in the world, consistently reminded humanity of the vision and the possibility of, in Pope Paul's words, "building a world where every man, no matter what his race, religion, or nationality, can live a fully human life, free from servitude imposed upon him by other men or by natural forces over which he has not sufficient control."

Assuming, as we unfortunately must, that many nations enslaved by avarice will not voluntarily relinquish even their superfluous material goods, it becomes necessary to spell out the ways by which the Third World can force the affluent areas of the world to assist the undernourished and illiterate millions. It seems almost inevitable that the nations of Africa, for example, will somehow unite and threaten the rich countries, including America, with a rain of intercontinental ballistic missiles if these wealthy nations continue to deny to Africans a truly human standard of living. Such a form of "blackmail" is by no means fanciful when one considers the fantastic power of the angry mobs which precipitated the French Revolution and the oppressed serfs who brought about the revolution in Russia. The newly emerged nations of the Third World, having driven the colonial powers out of their territory, will sooner than later demand massive reparations and indemnification for all the wealth which those powers "stole" from their "subjects." Massive resistance by the former colonial powers is a foregone conclusion. To think that the new nations will not resort to the sophisticated methods of making war developed by their former overlords is an illusion which no individual, no church, and no government should entertain.

As we can see from the foregoing paragraphs, the proponents of an entirely new foreign policy for America, predicated on at least $50 billion per year of foreign aid, have in their favor arguments beyond the basic morality and the Christian inspiration of their plan. At the same time those who would initiate a new and dramatic foreign policy, which would seek to attack communism at its very roots and causes, must do battle against the countless arrogant assumptions which prompted the decision to land ten thousand marines in the Dominican Republic in May 1965. One would hope that we have seen the last of this type of American military intervention to stop what was, rightly or wrongly, deemed to be an attempt by Communists and Castroites to infiltrate the government by the bid of Juan Bosch to regain power in that nation.

One would hope also that the nation's involvement in the Vietnam War would indicate to an ever-growing number of citizens that a land and air war in an underdeveloped country can seldom if ever bring peace and stability either to that country or to the United States.

Notes

1. (New York: Simon & Schuster, 1968).
2. *Ibid.*
3. *Ibid.*
4. *Ibid.*
5. (New York: Doubleday & Company, Inc., 1958), vol. 2, p. 231.

11.

Does America Make War Against Communism or on Behalf of Capitalism?

THE FEAR which Americans have had with respect to communism since the end of the Second World War has never been amenable to rational argument; it has been so pervasive and widespread that no national political figure has ever tried to minimize the almost theological horror of communism in all its forms which has become the hallmark of the loyal American.

Religious persons—and particularly Catholics—have assumed the posture of an almost brainwashed personality by the shrillness of their rhetoric which imputes persecution, inquisition, and violence to "world communism." Seldom, if ever, do Christians note that there is hardly a crime that can be attributed to Communists which they have not learned from Christians. Even the irenic tone of Pope John's *Pacem in Terris,* and the almost radical thrust of Pope Paul's encyclical on the development of nations, have done little to diminish the pervasiveness of the powerful myth that the communist monolithic monster is prepared to take over any capitalistic country by any means available.

A certain, almost evangelistic, anticommunism, exemplified by John Foster Dulles, still dominates the American mind even though the simplistic explanations of America's foreign policy during the Eisenhower administration have now been succeeded in intellectual circles by a much more sophisticated analysis of the relationships of nations within and beyond the communist world. In official American thinking about foreign policy today, there is a suppressed assumption that Americans somehow have a monopoly on moral and political virtue and wisdom and that it is America's high destiny to communicate this virtue and wisdom to all the nations of the globe.

Catholics have probably contributed more to American anticommunism than any other group in the United States. During the last four generations communism has been officially anathematized by the Holy See no less than twelve times. From Pius IX through Leo XIII and up to Pius XI, the condemnations of communism were so vehement that many observers felt that no way whatever was left in which it was permissible for Catholics to cooperate or to countenance communism in any form. Even a cursory examination of history reveals, however, that the Church was silent when Karl Marx evolved a piercing analysis of the real condition of a capitalistic society and discovered that only a radical breakup of the socioeconomic structure could put an end to the miseries of the proletariat. It is easy to say now that Marxism, while seeking to abolish the inhumane social and economic conditions of the working classes, fell into another extreme of inhumanity by a new form of totalitarianism. But Catholic thinking during the past century and today has never credited Marx with speaking out, when the Churches were silent, and demanding an economic and social order which would be worthy of man's material and mental aspirations. Nor have Catholics been able or willing to recognize that Pope Leo XIII's encyclical, *Rerum Novarum,* which appeared in 1891—just forty-three years after the Communist Manifesto—did *not* actually seek social reform but was, rather, an attempt at accommodation within the capitalistic structure. It was not until 1961, when the encyclical *Mater et Magistra* appeared, that some of the basic concepts of capitalism, such as the ownership of the means of production by private individuals, was called into question.

Because of the thunderous condemnation of communism in any form by Pope Pius XI during the 1930's, it became, among American Catholics and many other Christians, the undisputed greatest enemy of the Church or of Christianity. The fear generated by repeated and unsophisticated papal teaching against communism undoubtedly contributed to the fear which gripped all Americans in the late 1940's that there would be a communist take-over of the entire world. This fear, which cannot be validated by Marxist teachings or authenticated by the doctrines or practices of the Soviet Union, persists nonetheless to this day, and is to a large extent the underpinning of all American foreign policy.

One can only speculate on the extent to which American Catholics, in making up their minds about America's foreign policy, reasoned that what is good for the Catholic Church is also good for American foreign policy. Similarly, one can only wonder about the number of American Christians who endorsed a crusade by their nation against Communists because the occupation of a particular country by Communists would make it more difficult, or impossible, for Christian missionaries to operate in that land.

It is incredible that Americans have never really had a great national debate about the advisability, feasibility, and wisdom of a foreign policy born out of fear and dedicated to the containment of communism.

Many Americans would comment, of course, that the invasion by the Soviet Union of Czechoslovakia in 1968 made such a national debate unnecessary. The ruthlessness of Russia's tactics in Czechoslovakia, which repeated the Soviet assault on Hungary in 1956, may or may not be deemed to have been the result of Marxist or communist theory. But even if they were, the impotence of America's foreign policy is made manifest once again by the inability of the United States to prevent or roll back the unconscionable aggression against the two countries. In such an instance the thermonuclear shield of NATO is without value; and the vast numbers of American troops in Europe cannot be deployed to protect the people of Czechoslovakia or Hungary because, presumably, America has never been able to make commitments to any of the communist satellites to respond to their governments' pleas for assistance against an outside aggressor.

A more realistic statement of America's foreign policy would clearly indicate that the government will assist any nation which seeks American help to keep out a foreign aggressor, whether that aggressor be communist, fascist, or democratic. The proponents of America's existing foreign policy deny that they favor one form of government over another. After all the rhetoric denouncing communist intervention or foreign aggression has been employed, however, they admit that what they really want is to create or to preserve governments which are friendly to the United States.

If one assumes that the principal objective of America's foreign policy is to keep all forms of unfriendly governments out of the territory of prospective allies, then one must raise the question of whether the United States prefers capitalism over any other economic system. A prominent socialist theory of war suggests that all wars are attributable to the thinking and objectives of the industrialists in the nation which makes war. This sentiment has a good deal of evidence behind it including the statement of Woodrow Wilson that "the seed of war in the modern world is commercial and industrial rivalry."

Is it correct to state, therefore, that one of the reasons— perhaps a principal reason—for America's foreign policy is to win and hold foreign markets and to monopolize sources of raw materials against a noncapitalistic empire which, if it reaches these markets and raw materials, will almost inevitably cause the capitalistic nations to shrink and even to be eliminated?

The theory that America's foreign policy is based largely on a desire to preserve capitalism becomes more credible when one considers that the disintegration of the international despotism of communism is proceeding in an unpredictable but inevitable way.

It is arguable that the brutally enforced industrialization of an agrarian Russian culture in the Stalin era turned the Cold War into a massive struggle between the Soviet economy and the American economy. In this view of things the Cold War is not a struggle between a country possessed of the Marxist vision of the dictatorship of the proletariat against a free, democratic, and capitalistic society; rather, it is a struggle between Russia—seeking to industrialize as rapidly as possible—and the West, which has already achieved a high degree of industrialization and has possibly passed the zenith of its growth. Regardless, however, of the particular theory by which one chooses to explain the profound rivalry between the Soviet Union and the United States, it is unrealistic and untrue to describe the total confrontation in terms of the Marxist countries seeking to dominate the liberal democracies of the world.

In view of the substantial doubt concerning the ideological content of communist imperialism, is it therefore not incumbent and imperative for the United States to clarify and, if necessary, reverse its foreign policy? This would seem indicated if that policy is in fact predicated on a philosophy that it is the right of the United States to enter into war and to kill countless individuals in order to protect its economic and materialistic interests by retaining and extending the frontiers of American capitalism.

A few leftist or radical youths have commenced seriously to question the continued viability of capitalism in its American form. More and more these young persons agree with Woodrow Wilson who said: "The masters of the government of the United States are the combined capitalists and manufacturers of the United States." Yet it is simplistic to state that the industrial-military complex has exaggerated and even fabricated the existence of communism as a world threat to the United States. At the same time, the industrial powers in America—aided by many others—have created a fear of communism which makes all rational thought about it impossible.

The fusion of anticommunist sentiments with the voice and power of American industrialists invariably results in decisions which spell out the continuation and even the extension of the arms race. In November 1969, for example, Gov. Nelson A. Rockefeller of New York filed an extensive report regarding American policy toward the twenty-six nations in Latin America. The report noted, at least by implication, the alliance between the industrial and governmental interests of the United States, as well as the deep resentment in Latin America over the manner in which programs had been very often "distorted to serve a variety of purposes in the United States having nothing to do with the aspirations and interests of its neighbors." As an example of this alliance, the report called attention to the fact that at least half of all of the goods bought with aid funds must be transported in ships of the United States—an open subsidy to the shipping industry which takes up one-fifth of all of the aid given to the Western Hemisphere; it was recommended that this practice be abandoned.

Though the Rockefeller report stresses that the United States must in its own self-interest reaffirm and actually implement its unfulfilled pledge to make the hemisphere a better place for all Americans to live in, it nonetheless urges America not to turn down requests from the more industrialized Latin American nations for modern military equipment. Despite the fact that Latin America now spends a smaller percentage of its gross national product on defense than any other area of the world except certain nations of Africa, the Rockefeller report states that some Latin American nations will in fact be purchasing sophisticated military hardware from some source; therefore the United States should, in its own interest, be one of the suppliers. This recommendation is tied in with the prediction that, although there is now only one Castro in the hemisphere, there "can well be more in the future."

Yet, if the United States follows this recommendation, it will once again adopt a policy of keeping an equilibrium in the quantity and quality of arms when insurgents, revolutionaries, or Communists are threatening the stability of an existing government. Such a policy clearly does not go to the roots of the revolutionaries' grievances which, in Latin America, are the problems of population, poverty, unemployment, illiteracy, and injustice.

In November 1969 President Nixon incorporated some of the recommendations of the Rockefeller report in various statements. The melange of anticommunism, isolationism, and sheer capitalism which makes up American foreign policy was as manifest in the Nixon pronouncements as in the report. The president, for example, stated that the United States government would accept the existence of military governments in Latin America without subjecting them to a critical analysis of a moral nature. No attempt was made in making this statement to determine why or how a fascist, authoritarian regime is less dangerous to the United States than a communist regime. The assumption apparently is that all communist regimes are a part of a well-organized world-wide communist conspiracy and that one Castro is much more dangerous to the United States than any number of fascist regimes in the other twenty-five nations of the continent which is nearest to America.

The union of anticommunism with the aggressive capitalism of America has resulted in the situation which is described in the Rockefeller report as follows;

> The United States has all too often demonstrated, at least subconsciously, a paternalistic attitude toward other nations of the hemisphere. It has tried to direct the internal affairs of other nations to an unseemly degree, thinking, perhaps arrogantly, that it knew what was best for them. The United States has talked about partnership, but it has not truly practiced it.

Another mistake made in November 1969 as a result of the American anticommunist "mind-set" was the view taken by the Nixon administration not to seek an immediate freeze in the Helsinki Strategic Arms Limitation Talks (SALT) on tests for MIRV (Multiple Independently Targetable Reentry Vehicle). This latest horrible contribution of technology to the capacity of the human race to destroy itself is a kind of space bus which is designed to drop one nuclear warhead after another on one city after another in a single launching. Every delay in discussing the possibility of a moratorium on tests of this new weapon makes it more probable that the tests will in fact occur and that deployment by either the United States and/or Russia will follow.

The complexities behind the struggle over MIRV are likely to inhibit the vast majority of people from pronouncing on the question. At the governmental level human inertia, bureaucratic rigidity, and vested interests would appear to be so powerful that any reversal of direction in the upward trend in the arms race seems improbable.

In confrontation with this massive fact most Christians and

others, horrified by the prospect of even one more limited war like Vietnam, feel voiceless and powerless. The least that Christians and others could do, however, would be to rethink completely the verbal thunderbolts which they leveled at communism in all its forms in the past. Parallel with this serious obligation is a duty on the part of the Churches to reexamine and reject those elements of capitalism which enslave Americans in inane and trivial luxuries and imprison the peoples of the Third World in poverty, sickness, and illiteracy.

The Christian Churches and other religious bodies have made several pleas for a reasoned analysis of the nature of the "enemy" in the Vietnam War. Some Church units have pointed out that not all members of the Viet Cong or the National Liberation Front are in fact doctrinaire Communists. I, myself, found that in South Vietnam at least a few Catholics—and perhaps an increasing number—are members of the NLF. I also found in Paris that those associated with the Provisional Revolutionary government there feel more confident than does anyone in South Vietnam that a significant number of South Vietnamese Catholics would in fact approve of the ten points proposed by the NLF as a basis for settlement of the war.

The really tragic fact of the whole matter is that, even if it could be demonstrated that a majority of the Viet Cong were not actually Marxists or Communist in any significant way, the United States would still continue to categorize them as the "enemy," and the mass media in America would continue their uncritical and very dangerous policy of naming everyone in the Viet Cong and all persons in North Vietnam as "Communists."

United States policy in South Vietnam has become so hard-lined that any person opposed to the existing government, or any political faction—however noncommunist—which is opposed to President Thieu and Premier Ky, must simply be dismissed as a part of the "Enemy" apparatus. It sometimes appears that the United States would have to make Communists of all of the Viet Cong even if they were not Communists! It may be, moreover, that the attractiveness of communism is increased for the one-half of humanity which makes its home in Asia by the instinctive revulsion most people feel toward a powerful nation, possessed of superior weapons, which is killing poorly armed combatants and defenseless civilians of another race in a backward country.

One wonders how long the mystique of anticommunism can unite the American people to arm themselves to the teeth and to inflict war, where necessary, to prevent any group of individuals who even sound like Communists from unsettling the international political status quo. It is the undeniable duty of the Churches and religious groups in America to detheologize the war on communism and to state unequivocally that the differences in the economic theories about property between Marxism and capitalism do not justify international armed conflict, however such conflict may be rationalized and moralized.

12.

American Unilateralism, the United Nations, and World Federalism

THE STATED POLICY of the United States is to drive out "bad" Communist governments and to replace them with "good" democratic, capitalistic regimes. Robert Heilbroner, in 1967, wrote that "our present policy prefers the absence of development to the chance for communism—which is to say that we prefer hunger and want and the existing inadequate assaults against the causes of hunger and want to any regime that declares its hostility to capitalism."[1]

The primary motivation behind America's crusade against revolution is presumably an idealistic desire to save the people of Africa, Asia, and Latin America from the horrors of Stalinism; but the major premises behind such a crusade simply do not make sense to the inhabitants of the Third World. To these hundreds of millions of persons the United States has taken a position that any government different from the existing regime is likely to promote instability and, consequently, must be thwarted. Everyone will admit that communism may not have the answer to the problems of the economic development of poverty-impacted nations. Communist approaches to industrial development have sometimes been too dogmatic, too impractical, and too punitive to be successful. At the same time, is it not cruel and arrogant for the United States to prevent revolution on the theory that revolution in the end will turn out to be worse than starvation? In effect, American policy often sacrifices the reform of social institutions to the goal of anticommunism. Once again the assumption is that all revolutions are inspired by outside powers and that these revolutions are orchestrated by some powerful worldwide authority.

Is it not reasonable for the black and yellow peoples of Africa and Asia to think that the United States has a policy which is designed to prevent the expropriation by radical regimes of the billions of dollars of American corporate assets invested in the Third World? Is it not understandable that the citizens of the nonindustrialized nations can see the fear of the United States of confrontation with the rise of the developing nations to international visibility? Is it not understandable, moreover, that the nations, which the United States in its paternalistic way seeks to retain in the Free World, look upon the United States as a power whose military involvement is impossible to reconcile with any global campaign to preserve true freedom?

What, for example, can the people of Africa think of the United States when it affirms its concern for the material advance of all men and the prosperity of democratic values, but allows and even encourages American corporations to benefit by the labor of 12 million black people who are the culture slaves of the fascism of some 3.5 million whites? In South Africa whites have the fourth highest standard of living in the world, while in the same nation every third black child dies of undernourishment before it is a year old, and 60 percent of all blacks live below the breadline. Oppression of blacks in South Africa continues to intensify in every form. In 1965, for example, out of 3.4 million whites 33,000 attended universities; out of 12 million blacks only 946 attended universities.

Other examples can be cited of the United States keeping communism out of the Free World while presiding over the further impoverishment of these nations. Paraguay, Haiti, Venezuela, Liberia, and the Dominican Republic are familiar examples of countries with a pathetically low per capita income but with extensive operations by American corporations bringing profit to absentee stockholders in the United States while preventing any true radical social reform in the countries where these profits originate.

The manner in which the United States executes this foreign policy is also, quite understandably, considered outrageous by the nations which America seeks to keep in the Free World. This policy is deemed to be imperialism or, at best, unilateralism, both of which inevitably lead to militarism. Consequently the policy decision made by the United States twenty-five years ago—to oppose all regimes in the Third World calling themselves communist or which seem to be leaning toward communism—is one which appears to be drawing together revolutionary leaders of the Third World who are joined together only by their common fear and hatred of the United States. American foreign policy is, in other words, furnishing what Marxism-Leninism had failed to offer to the revolutionary movements—an ideological bond to bring together the nationalist revolutionary movements spread across three continents.

If, therefore, the United States continues to make it a policy to oppose nationalism wherever it is intermingled with a radical political and economic program, it must expect to be hated and feared by political leaders who will eventually speak for a majority of the population of the world. The

United States, in addition, will be increasingly charged with inconsistencies in the application of the combination of principles by which its foreign policy is formulated. The Chinese invasion of Tibet, for example, was ignored by the United States even though the violent seizure of power in that country by an external communist regime was a much clearer case of communist aggression than was the case of Greece or Vietnam. Apparently one of the reasons for the decision by the United States not to intervene in Tibet was the fear of provoking a war with China.

The United States, furthermore, has not made the violent character of a government's accession to power the test for American intervention. Military coups which have seized power from constitutional regimes have been rather regularly recognized and supported. For example, military takeovers in Argentina (1955), Turkey (1961), Burma (1962), Indonesia (1966), and Ghana (1966) have received the "blessing" of the United States government. The worldwide pattern of United States military involvement therefore cannot be said to form any consistent global campaign to preserve freedom. It has not been a broad based campaign to defend freedom against totalitarianism.

Nor is it certain that those nations in which the United States has intervened, during the twenty years since the Truman Doctrine was announced, are now any more economically and politically stronger than those which have not witnessed an intervention by America. For example, in Guatemala, Iran, Indonesia, and the Congo—all of which have experienced major United States intervention designed to change the politics of the country—no notable progress towards the goals of democracy, stability, and economic progress has been achieved.

There is, of course, nothing new about powerful countries asserting the nationalistic or imperial prerogative of using coercion on the territory of another nation without that nation's consent. Most empires in the course of human history have asserted the right to control the politics of other peoples in the name of a moral idea such as the "Free World." Athens offered civilization, Rome offered the blessings of its imperial law, and Britain proffered the power and prestige of its empire. The United States, having assumed "responsibility" for all of the nations in the Free World, has merely acted in its turn like most powerful nations have always acted in the past.

The most disastrous and devastating result of this policy, by which the United States has acted in the imperial mold, is the implicit erosion of the United Nations. The United States, in other words, has increasingly claimed the unilateral right to determine whether a conflict anywhere in the world constitutes a threat to the national security of America. The inherent power of America constitutes the basis of the legitimacy of this claim. In his widely acclaimed book entitled *Intervention and Revolution,* Richard J. Barnet, an expert on insurgent movements around the world, asserts that "the architects of United States foreign policy have developed a rationale to justify global intervention which ... is inconsistent with the multilateralism of the United Nations charter and the dictates of traditional international law."[2]

The passing of each year makes it more impossible for the United States to give up this way of acting in the world. The primary allegiance of the president and the Congress is to serve the national interest. On virtually every issue the "national interest" which elected officials are committed to serve is seen by the military, the corporations, and the labor unions not as an abstract "world community" but as a basic military and economic help of the United States. There is no constituency in America, in other words, to lobby for the removal of the grossest inequalities among the developed and underdeveloped nations. The two or three million American citizens who live abroad cannot in the nature of things establish or make up such a constituency since they have a vested interest in keeping the American posture in the nation where they reside almost exactly as it is.

The United Nations charter rests on the basic principle that the preservation of international peace and the protection of the security of each member nation is a matter for multilateral decision. It may be that the charter was compromised from the very beginning by the apparently unavoidable placing of responsibility in the hands of the major powers which were given permanent seats on the Security Council. But the United States has followed a policy of bypassing the United Nations for so many years that virtually no one now raises the question which Adlai Stevenson, shortly before his death, put in these words: "It is time to decide whether we are going to be international and multilateral or not."

American officials have, of course, dealt with this charge of unilateralism on many occasions. One approach to an answer is the common assertion that the criminal elements of the world have made any true multilateral structure impossible and that consequently the United States, by opposing these criminal elements, is actually working to create a world where multilateral decision making will be possible. Another attempt at countering the charge of unilateralism is the American involvement in regional groups such as the Organization of American States (OAS). The fact is, however, that in virtually all of these multilateral organizations the United States begins or ends up as the dominant power with all other nations taking a subservient role.

The Catholic Reaction to American Nationalism

One of the great tragedies in American Catholicism in 1970 is that practically no one recognizes that the United States has been consistently violating the fundamental principles of world solidarity and of the family of nations elaborated by the papacy over a long period and developed by Catholic theologians and philosophers since at least the day of Suarez. It is unfortunate indeed that the American Catholic bishops, meeting in Washington in November 1969, said nothing about Vietnam, peace, or the urgent need for the United States to work actively and militantly to strengthen the United Nations, in order that the twenty-year period of American unilateralism in world affairs might change its course in a radical way. Although the bishops' meeting was held just before Moratorium Day (November 15), which brought to the nation's capital the largest demonstration in the history of America, the bishops did not look ahead to the end of the Vietnam War or urge, even in the most general principles, the creation of a world community along the lines of the supranational federation which the last four popes have urged in the strongest terms.

In short, there appears to be virtually no background work being done by the bishops to produce a 'blueprint' for the foreign policy of America during the 1970's. This lack of action is decidedly unlike that which took place during the last several months of World War II; at that time the American bishops, with the aid of many experts and the now defunct Catholic Association for International Peace, developed extraordinarily progressive statements on what the United States and the United Nations should do at the end of the war.

It seems worthwhile to quote a part of the statement made by the American bishops on November 18, 1945. While not as bold and clear as papal statements before and since that time, it speaks as follows:

> The charter which emerged from the San Francisco Conference, while undoubtedly an improvement on the Dumbarton Oaks proposals, does not provide for a sound, institutional organization of the international society. The Security Council provisions make it no more than a virtual alliance of the great Powers for the maintenance of peace. These nations are given

a status above the law. Nevertheless, our country acted wisely in deciding to participate in this world organization. It is better than world chaos. ... In time ... we may have a sound institutional organization of the international community which will develop, not through mere voluntary concessions of the nations, but from the recognition of the rights and duties of international society.[3]

This is a far less specific statement than the famous 1944 Christmas address of Pius XII on democracy in which he had urged that there be an international body "with supreme authority and with power to smother in its germinal stages any threat of isolated or collective aggression." Nor have the Catholic bishops since 1945 ever approached the unqualified endorsement which Pope Pius XII gave to the ideal of world federalism. In 1951, for example, Pius XII, speaking to the leaders of the movement for world federalism and knowing that they advocated the transformation of the United Nations by charter revision into a form of world government, subscribed to the movement in these words:

> Your movement dedicates itself to realizing an effective political organization of the world. Nothing is in more conformity with the traditional doctrine of the Church. ... It is necessary therefore to arrive at an organization of this kind, if for no other reason than to put a stop to the armament race. ...

It is perhaps significant to note that in 1953 the then Monsignor Montini, now Pope Paul VI, writing in the name of the Holy Father to the *Semaines Sociales* meeting in France, rebuked those Catholics who were insensitive to admonitions of the papacy. Montini's letter read: "How many ... continue to shut themselves up within the narrow confines of a chauvinistic nationalism, incompatible with the courageous effort to start a world community *demanded* by recent popes" (emphasis added).

In December 1956 Pius XII, after witnessing a broken

Hungary and an exploding Middle East, wrote with unusual
directness:

> This organization [the United Nations] ought also to have the
> right and power of forestalling all military intervention of one
> state in another, whatever be the pretext under which it is
> effected, and also the right and power of assuming, by means
> of a sufficient police force, the safeguarding of order in a state
> which is threatened.

From these citations and many others it is clear beyond
doubt that Pius XII was an unabashed internationalist and
that he desired and advocated a supranational juridical world
order which could, for example, proscribe atomic, biological,
and chemical warfare; more importantly, it would modify the
sovereignty of each nation of the earth and thereby give
juridical enforceability to the unity of mankind.

The two pontiffs who have succeeded Pius XII have reiterated his plea for world government in various ways and have
possibly strengthened the Catholic doctrine of the family of
nations—a doctrine and a tradition whose depths and riches
are set forth in a classic volume on the subject by John Eppstein, *Catholic Tradition of the Law of Nations.**

The general failure of American Catholics to follow the
challenging leadership of the papacy in urging a world government is more difficult to understand in view of Pius XII's
statement that

> Catholics ... are extraordinarily well-equipped to collaborate
> in the creation of a climate without which a common action
> on the international plane can have neither substance nor
> prosperous growth. ... There is no other group of human beings so favorably disposed, in breadth and in depth, for international understanding. ... Catholics ... above all ... must
> realize that they are called to overcome every vestige of nationalistic narrowness. ...

*London: Burns, Oates and Washbourne Ltd., 1935.

Why is it that American Catholics, generally so faithful in carrying out the mandates of the Holy See, have neglected papal teaching on the international order almost to the point of defiance? Why is it that Catholics in America have made virtually no protest against the unilateralism implicit in American foreign policy during the past twenty years—a unilateralism which undercuts the United Nations and which is contrary to all of the explicit and implicit directives of the Holy See with regard to what Catholics should be doing to promote the solidarity of the world community?

Catholic bishops in Europe and elsewhere have acquiesced in the nationalism which has been the curse of the modern world since the rise of the sovereign nation-state. The Catholic bishops of America have apparently succumbed to the same temptation and have given little guidance to the almost one-fourth of the nation which professes fidelity to Catholicism. It is exciting to contemplate what changes would take place in American foreign policy if the majority of American Catholics, by word and by deed, insisted that their nation abstain from unilateralism and worked mightily to transform the United Nations into a world government with the one source of military power.

It is discouraging beyond description that the American Catholic bishops in November 1969 said not one word about the prophetic role which American Catholics should and must play to persuade the nation that the foreign policy which it now pursues in the name of anticommunism will not in fact contain communism; will not assure peace, but will only postpone and perhaps make impossible the attainment of a world government which is compelled by Catholic doctrine and which alone can bring about some semblance of peace in the international quarter.

It is even more discouraging to contemplate the possibility that American Catholics, having been disillusioned by papal statements concerning birth control and other matters, may also question the credibility of the Holy See when it pleads for world federalism, the surrender of a certain portion of each nation's sovereignty, and the pooling of some of the material resources and all of the military potential of all of the nations of the earth in one supranational agency.

Notes

1. *Commentary* (April 1967).
2. (New York: New American Library, Inc., 1968), p. 260.
3. National Catholic Welfare Conference pamphlet (1945).

13.

America's Lawlessness in the Conduct of the Vietnam War

IT SHOULD BE CLEAR from the foregoing that the anticommunist and procapitalist motivation which undergirds America's foreign policy has not consistently been applied to deter communism; moreover, it is doing very little to bring industrialization to the eighty underdeveloped nations who are members of the World Bank. Unless something enormously dramatic happens in the relationship between the rich and the poor nations, the undeveloped countries can hope for only a per capita income at the end of this century of $170 a year. In 1968 the per capita income of the United States was $2,700, with an anticipated rise to at least $4,500 by the year 2000.

Not only is American foreign policy not "containing" communism as its central purpose suggests but, to repeat, it is, more disastrously, undermining the brightest hope of mankind in the nuclear age, the United Nations.

In response to all these contentions, the defenders of America's bipartisan foreign policy nonetheless maintain that the United States must continue to fulfill the commitments which it has made over the past generation to threescore nations across the globe. It is contended in this chapter that the wars for which the United States has prepared itself cannot be waged, much less be carried to a successful conclusion, under the existing rules of international law pertaining to the conduct of armed conflict between nations. In other words it is the thesis of this chapter that the United States, in pursuing its policy of preventing the spread of communism, has actually prepared the armed forces of the nation to engage in wars in which massive lawlessness will be endemic and inevitable.

Conceding, for the moment therefore, that a war designed to prevent a communist take-over of a particular nation might be successful in achieving its objective, such a war nonetheless would inevitably violate those rules of war which represent the collective voice and conscience of civilized humanity.

A study entitled *In the Name of America,** demonstrates by a collection of some twelve hundred clippings and other documents that the conduct of the war in Vietnam by the armed forces of the United States has frequently manifested a defiance of the laws of war regarding the care of the sick and wounded, the rights of noncombatants, and the plight of refugees. This massive and unimpeachable documentation of reprehensible conduct on the part of American forces in South Vietnam suggests, and possibly proves, that similar conduct would be essential for the waging of any other guerrilla war in the nations whose territorial integrity the United States is committed to protect. In view, therefore, of this new legal-moral dilemma, it may be helpful to review the rules of war which the United States, because of ignorance, heedless-

*New York: E.P. Dutton & Co., Inc., 1968.

ness, or malice has frequently violated in the war in Vietnam.

The *Constitution on the Church* of the Second Vatican Council, having stated flatly that it is the "clear duty" of Christians "to strain every muscle" to mount a war on war, went on to remark that the international covenants regarding the rules of war to which a large number of nations have subscribed "*must* be honored" (emphasis added).

The international treaties to which Vatican II made reference were the Hague Convention of 1907 and the four Geneva Conventions of 1929 and 1949. Vatican II also included, by implicit reference, the principles established at the International Court in Nuremberg, a tribunal whose basic decisions were unanimously affirmed by the General Assembly of the United Nations on December 11, 1946. The principles of Nuremberg, later formulated by the United Nations with the express approval of the United States, defined as "war crimes" certain "violations of the laws or customs of war which include ill treatment of prisoners of war" or the "wanton destruction of cities, towns, or villages." The following observations about these rules of war are significant:

1. The rules of war as spelled out in the Hague and Geneva conventions are the supreme law of the land under the American Constitution. These rules apply to all wars, including guerrilla warfare, in which a signatory such as the United States is in any way a party.

2. The rules of war are not suspended for a party to a war even if the belligerent nation totally disregards them. Specific reprisals may on occasion be made to counter an enemy assault, but even the most illegal conduct on the part of the enemy does not justify an abandonment of the rules of war by the other party to the conflict.

3. The only justification for noncompliance with any of the rules of war is the claim that observance of the rules of warfare is rendered impossible by the "necessities of war."

The book, *In the Name of America*, makes it unmistakably

clear that the American forces in South Vietnam have indulged in conduct which can be justified only by recourse to the inherently expandable defense of "military necessity." Those who would justify the conduct of America in South Vietnam must, in effect, indicate that the rules of war are either no longer realistic in guerrilla warfare or that they are eroded, if not eviscerated, by the loosely phrased excusing clause of "military necessity."

If Americans look at the facts clearly, they must confess that the United States government has followed a pattern of lawlessness in Vietnam and presumably feels that such a course is an essential prerequisite to the attainment of America's stated purposes in the Vietnam struggle.

The unavoidable legal-moral question which any defender of the Vietnam War must confront comes to this: Can any stated policy for America's activities in Vietnam—whether it be to defend the United States or to save South Vietnam from communist aggression—be justified if the *only strategy* to achieve such a policy contains within it as a "military necessity" the need to violate those minimal standards for the conduct of warfare agreed to by all the world's civilized nations in the Hague-Geneva conventions? By what moral norm, in other words, can the United States expect to keep South Vietnam in the Free World when it pursues a course of conduct in which, in violation of the Universal Rules of War, it acquiesces to the inhumane treatment of prisoners by South Vietnamese officials, the destruction of the "enemy" by its own mobile medical units, the defoliation of crops, and the devastation of arable lands?

There is no world tribunal where charges that a nation has violated international law by disregarding the rules of war may be heard and passed upon. But the whole of Asia has already heard and will continue to hear for many years to come about America's indiscriminate killing of civilians, the hardships which it imposed on noncombatants, and the total inadequacy of American attempts to alleviate civilian hardships in Vietnam.

When I walked the streets of Saigon or inspected the devastated areas outside that city, I could think of nothing except the words of Vatican II, which spoke of modern warfare as nothing but "reciprocal slaughter." I thought also of the words of that Council, when the twenty-two hundred bishops of the world urged all of humanity to "praise those who renounce the use of violence in the vindication of their rights."

In the Name of America, which was commissioned and published by the peace group, Clergy and Laymen Concerned About Vietnam, produced no reaction at the Pentagon except a routine denial that the military forces in Vietnam had consciously or otherwise violated the rules of war which, the Pentagon release pointed out carefully, were spelled out in the handbooks issued to each American combat soldier.

In view of the sheer irrationality of modern war, perhaps we should be grateful that the American government *has* manifested some restraint in Vietnam. America has, after all, not bombed the dikes in North Vietnam or employed atomic weapons or allowed its tremendous military power to be employed unchecked. But the fact remains that America has utilized its overwhelming military strength in Vietnam in ways which simply cannot be in compliance with the fundamental aspects of the rules of war. The officials at the Pentagon have not even taken refuge in the simple fact that the Hague-Geneva rules for the conduct of war are simplistic to the point of being obsolete. American military officials have, instead, continued to deceive the American people and have attempted to justify all aspects of America's intervention in Vietnam by the bromide that all war produces excruciatingly difficult circumstances; consequently it is impossible to mitigate the inhumane aspects of modern warfare.

It is not farfetched to predict that there will be a Nuremberg trial in South Vietnam or in Southeast Asia in which the United States will be tried and convicted for many if not all of the atrocities alleged to have been committed by the Green Berets and by other military officials seeking some type of a reprisal or merely carrying out a "search and destroy" mission. Americans will discount all such trials much as they dismissed the allegedly communist-inspired trials of Stockholm in which the United States was found guilty of an immoral and illegal war in Southeast Asia.

Regardless, however, of American sentiment with regard to the almost inevitable Nuremberg-type trials to be held in Asia, the fact is that most Asians—and perhaps most Americans—will believe virtually all of the atrocities imputed to American soldiers by an all-Asian tribunal which will sit in judgment on the most powerful nation in the history of the world after the agony of Vietnam has been terminated.

On the assumption that America's experience in the Vietnam war proves rather conclusively that America cannot carry out its commitments to other nations without a massive violation of the rules of war, is there then any way by which America may continue its present foreign policy without implicitly stating to the entire world that it is prepared to enter on a path of lawlessness in order to achieve the objective of keeping the poor and underdeveloped nations out of the communist sector of the world?

Aside from the actual lawlessness involved in any intervention by the United States in a war between that nation and allegedly communist aggressors, one has to wonder what the continued use of violence does to the conscience of America. The employment of violence, like the continued return to sin, silences the conscience of those who engage in it and those who observe it. It is clear at this time that the violence in South Vietnam, together with the concomitant lawlessness, has escalated the inherent arrogance which Americans, like all other powerful peoples, have towards the last, the lowest, and the least of humanity.

America's record in dishonoring the minimal constraints that civilized people have agreed upon as necessary in the waging of war constitutes one more compelling reason to believe what Pope John said in *Pacem in Terris* that it is "irrational to believe that war is still an apt means of vindicating violated rights."

America's failure to observe the rules of war in Vietnam must remind everyone of the principles which governed the prosecution of the Nazi leaders at Nuremberg. These principles, as restated by the United Nations, specifically note the fact that "complicity in the commission of a ... war crime ... is [in itself] a crime under international law."

Can American citizens ever hope that one of its future governments may admit to its constituents that American military and civilian personnel were guilty of complicity in the commission of crimes against the rules of war in Vietnam? Can Catholics hope and pray that the highest officials in the Church, after having surveyed the conduct of modern nations in guerrilla warfare, will state clearly and categorically that no such warfare may be engaged in because it unavoidably and inevitably requires the participants to engage in a form of defiance of international law which is of such a magnitude that any possible justification of the war is nullified because of the means employed to wage it?

If one desires to be honest about all war, therefore, it is necessary to state, as Vatican II has made clear, that all atomic war, whether offensive or defensive, is forbidden; and all guerrilla warfare involves so many violations of international law that it would seem to become immoral simply by reason of the illegal methods and procedures followed.

Does it then follow that the pacifist approach is the only moral option left open for the Christian? It is to that central and crucial question to which we now turn our attention.

14.

Is Pacifism the Only Option Left for Christians?

THE TERM "pacifist" has never had a very positive connotation among most Christians and perhaps particularly not among Catholics. If one advocates pacifism or even expresses sympathy with the idea, almost immediately virtually every Christian will ask if the speaker believes that each individual has a moral right to protect himself in the event that his life is threatened. It is somehow assumed that the pacifist must be an absolutist in that he is opposed to all use of force or violence to protect any objective. Every dictionary definition of "pacifist," however, stresses that the term has always been restricted to the use of "military" force. Despite this widely accepted definition of pacifism, there is nonetheless a rather universal resistance to the concept on the grounds that it is naive and unrealistic.

In a definitive book, *Pacifism in the United States, from the Colonial Era to the First World War,** Peter Brock treats all facets of pacifism. He concedes that, throughout most of the period he surveys, pacifists at their best constituted a small elite and at worst, an exclusive clique. At the same time Professor Brock indicates by his massive documentation that the pacifism of the Quakers, Mennonites, and other similar religious groups had an enormous impact on American society—an influence which may possibly be witnessing its flowering in the outcries from every social class and every age group which have made the war in Vietnam the most detested in American history.

Many theological strands entered into the formulation of American pacifism. The Anabaptists and the Mennonites denounce war basically because of their theological conceptions against what they conceive to be the tyranny of the state. In the 19th century and thereafter, pacifism in America tended to be essentially an optimistic creed which placed its faith in the eventual perfectibility of man.

The few Protestant theologians who have argued vigorously and consistently on behalf of pacifism are today more persuasive than most Christians would imagine. It may be that the chilling fear of the atomic mushroom, and our anguished nightmares about the horrors of Vietnam, precondition us to accept any line of argument which would ease our anxiety and guilt about the fundamental irrationality of the foreign policy which the United States has pursued for almost twenty-five years.

The theological sorites for pacifism is much more sophisticated than even well-informed Catholics might surmise. The theological defenders of pacifism do not rely upon any literalist or oversimplified version of Scripture to support their argument. Inevitably they rely upon Scripture, both the Old and the New Testaments, but they orchestrate this with

---

*Princeton, N.J.: Princeton University Press, 1968.

quotations from the early Christian Fathers and from theologians in almost every age of Christianity.

One's viewpoint on pacifism depends upon one's priorities concerning the ultimate objectives of organized society. In the inevitable disorder and violence which characterize all societies, if one starts with the premise that society's foremost objective is to minimize the number of deaths caused by social and political unrest and violence, it would appear to follow—especially since the advent of modern or total war—that almost any social or political calamity should be accepted; otherwise, any contrary policy would be inconsistent with the objective of minimizing the number of deaths at the hands of those who would overthrow or occupy a particular nation.

If on the other hand one starts with the premise that the preservation of the fundamental rights of peoples is on certain occasions an objective for which even the lives of men may be sacrificed, then pacifism is hardly a viable option. An appealing case can be made for the exaltation of the basic rights of human beings in the instance of genocide. The searing book, *While Six Million Died,* by Arthur D. Morse,* is a powerful document which indicts the United States, particularly the State Department, for appalling apathy and carelessness in the face of Nazi genocide.

If a person feels that the preservation of national borders or the protection of the social, political, or religious freedom of a nation-state justifies at least a defensive war, there is hardly any place at all in such a scheme of things for pacifism.

Of the three Christian positions with regard to war—pacifism, the just war, and the crusade—pacifism was undeniably *the* belief of the primitive Church and of the vast majority of Christians until Constantine. It would be enormously convenient if it could be proven that the early Church correctly interpreted the mind of the New Testament when it en-

*New York: Random House, Inc., 1968.

dorsed pacifism, and that the history of the Church since that period has been a progressive fall from a state of primitive purity. Such a conclusion would be reached too blithely, however, because there are other factors to explain the almost total absence of Christians of the early Church from the military and from participation in war. Furthermore, the mere fact that most Christians would have nothing to do with armed conflict does not necessarily prove that this was a doctrine or dogma of the early Church, just as the acquiescence in the institution of slavery by early Christians does not necessarily prove that they felt that this was a moral institution.

There is, nevertheless, rather overwhelming evidence that Tertullian, Lactantius, Origen, St. Clement of Alexandria, St. Cyprian, and many others made it clear that the early Church saw an incompatibility between Christian love and killing. The early Christians' aversion to killing was justified by a wide variety of explanations. Some theologians, like Tertullian and Origen, took the radical position that the empire was ordained because of sin and should be left to sinners. Others adopted a more pragmatic or redemptive type of pacifism. For these individuals, war was evil because there was a more excellent way.

There has been no significant literature in the Catholic tradition which would seek to prove that the early Church misinterpreted the Old and New Testaments and erred by abandoning the clear pacifist doctrine in the Bible. Catholic thinkers have not, for example, tried to develop into certainty the contention by some early Christian writers that there could be no justifiable war after the wars sanctioned by God himself and recorded in the Old Testament. Nor has there been any significant minority view in Catholic tradition to the effect that the early Christians compromised with the concept of war as embodied in Roman law. Christians of subsequent generations have, in general, followed the practice of the early Christians of neither condoning the sins of the state nor despising its benefits. Neither the early Church nor the vast majority of Christians through the ages have followed the Book of the Apocalypse in identifying Rome with anti-Christ. Most Christians in all ages have deemed a well-ordered temporal society as a providential provision for the dissemination of the Gospel. Such an attitude may, of course, lead to the endorsement by Christians of a particular secular order which allows them to spread the gospel—even if the preservation of such an arrangement requires armed conflict.

Adolph Harnack accused the Church of diluting the unrelenting opposition to war which the early Christians manifested in countless ways. While this accusation may be just, the real scandal is that modern Christians, even when confronted with the horrendous developments of modern war, do not revert to or evince the abhorrence of all war so manifest among the earliest Christians. As Father Francis Stratmann says:

> What would St. Paul have written if he had been confronted with the spirit of modern war and many of its developments such as poison gas? Who can doubt that he would have used his scourge against such war? When he wrote, there were no wars, great or little, going on. He wrote under the Pax Romana.[1]

Even though scholars and Christians will continue to debate about the existence and validity of pacifism in the New Testament and in early Christianity, the fact is that the Christians of the first three centuries constitute, by their lives and by their achievements, the greatest proof in all history that a nonviolent "war" of love is infinitely more powerful than the sword and is incapable of being destroyed by any armed conflict. They gave witness to the irreducible conflict between the nonviolent Christian and the tyranny of state absolutism. It is a form of pacifism which produced a long line of martyrs who submitted to the sword. And it was pacifism which, in the ultimate analysis, caused Constantine to recognize that Christianity could not be exterminated. He surrendered, not necessarily because of any genuine conversion or because Christians had become a majority (in the year 313 A.D. they were still a very small minority), but simply because he recognized that no amount of armed force could effectively deny to the Christian revolutionaries the right to exist in the Roman Empire.

This example of the early Christians, contrasted with the Cold War between the Soviet Union and the United States, forces the mind to the crucial question: Can or must a Catholic be a pacifist in the present situation? A Catholic *may,* of course, be a pacifist if he judges that the evidence of Christian history makes pacifism a live option for himself; a Christian *must* be a complete pacifist if his intellect has persuaded his conscience that this is the *only* option available to him since, in the ultimate analysis, the voice of conscience—as Martin Luther King and Cardinal Newman would agree—is the voice of God.

It may not be necessary, however, for most Christians to reach this absolute decision and to condemn all war under any conditions as immoral. The immorality of atomic warfare has been unequivocally condemned by Vatican II, and all conventional wars which might be waged in the modern world can hardly pass muster under the various requirements of the theory of the just war.

Even if one is a pacifist, however, either on the principle of the immorality of all wars or because one thinks that all possible modern wars are unjustifiable, such a position does not resolve all of the problems concerning the extent to which a Christian can cooperate in a society in which he is compelled by countless laws to contribute to the massive military preparations of his nation. About the only specific relief which the Second Vatican Council and the American bishops have given to persons opposed to modern war is the recommendation that the state give immunity, not merely to the pure pacifist but to the selective conscientious objector. Such immunity is still not available in the United States where there is compulsory peacetime military conscription—an institution against which all popes during the past century have inveighed.

The Christian in America who is opposed to all modern wars is required to pay federal taxes of which approximately 60 percent goes for some type of military preparedness. This is one reason why the actions by which some strike out at various manifestations of the military empire in America are understandable. The destruction of draft files by the Catonsville Nine, and similar actions by Christians in Milwaukee and elsewhere, may be a dramatic "homily" against the evils of militarism; and the sincerity and heroism of those who participate in such activities is beyond dispute. But for persons not inspired to engage in this type of prophetic witness, what is the most logical and effective way to be heard? What can be done to change the course of a nation, so blinded by the alleged evils of communism and its purported threat to the security of the nation, that it has become persuaded that it is a duty of patriotism to continue to support the national commitment to provide military solutions to social and economic problems around the globe?

I would suggest that the time has come for Christians, and particularly Catholics, to stop theorizing about the "possibility" of a just war, to take a realistic view that bilateral disarmament of the Soviet Union and the United States is highly improbable, and to start advocating a policy of passive resistance or militant nonviolence toward any nation which would seek to conquer America, seize our assets, and control our minds.

Following such an option would undoubtedly require unilateral risk and would, concededly, leave the American people open to a certain defenselessness against the new instruments of total destruction. It is appropriate to recall, however, that unilateral disarmament on the part of the United States would by no means necessarily result in a larger number of dead than would result if one or more of the other atomic powers, by accident or by design, launched a nuclear war on a fully armed America. Scientific leaders such as Dr. Edward Teller have estimated that in a nuclear war probably no more than 10 percent of the American population would be wiped out. Assuming, then, that some twenty million Americans would be killed in a "first strike" war launched by one of the nuclear nations, does it follow that such an attack becomes more probable if the United States tells the world that it has abandoned its policy of "massive retaliation" and that it has surrendered its policy of atomic "sufficiency" because it has realized that this is a policy of incitement as much as it is a policy of deterrence?

This suggested policy of nonviolence should not, however, be construed or dismissed as a passive surrender or a defeatist compliance with a foreign power thought to be a possible aggressor. The proposed alternative would openly confront the fact that the mutual terror which now exists between America and the Soviet Union is so hideous that no different arrangement could be worse.

The disarmament would be accompanied by a warning to the entire world that the American people will not be governed by any foreign power. If conquered by superior military force, they will become a totally ungovernable people who will drive out the aggressor by highly sophisticated techniques of nonviolence developed, if need be, with all of the fantastic resources which America now puts in the hands of its military complex. All these techniques of civil disobedience and noncooperation, which were used in Gandhi's movement, would be developed by the application of the discoveries which the behavioral sciences have unlocked with regard to motivation and the dynamics of morale.

The very thought of even partial unilateral disarmament is without doubt unthinkable to many, if not most people, in the United States. But on the assumption that the Russians and other potential "enemies" of America retain their sanity, there is literally no chance at all that any political authority would consciously choose to start a nuclear war. McGeorge Bundy, special assistant to two United States presidents on national security affairs, stated this conclusion in these words:

> Given the worst calculations of the most pessimistic American advocate of new weapon systems, there is no prospect at all that the Soviet government could attack the United States without incurring an overwhelming risk of destruction vastly greater than anyone but a madman would choose to accept.[2]

Mr. Bundy goes on to state that the "basic consequence of considering this matter politically and not technically is the conclusion that beyond a point long since past the escalation of the strategic nuclear race makes no sense for either the Soviet Union or the United States."[3] Although Mr. Bundy states in the same article that he feels that a "credible strategic nuclear deterrent is indispensable to the peace," he urges nonetheless that the president of the United States will find "solid support for the kind of reassessment that could lead to a decision that the United States, on its own, will take a small step away from the nuclear arms race." That small step, Mr. Bundy concludes, "could be a giant leap for mankind."[4]

Mr. Bundy does urge that the United States make a decision "on its own." The Christian who has come to the conclusion that neither nuclear nor guerrilla warfare is morally permissible has experts on the disarmament tangle, such as Mr. Bundy, agreeing with him, at least to the extent that the United States must take some initiative "on its own" if the nation believes in the "assumption of sanity" which is the basis of Mr. Bundy's argument.

Virtually no Christians in America, except the theologically oriented pacifist, advocate anything like the position noted above. Even the best-informed and most devout Christians dismiss unilateral disarmament as a virtual invitation to the Russians to destroy the nation. One of the very few Catholics to delve into the strategy of a "war by love," conducted by nonviolence or passive resistance, is Gordon Zahn, a former professor at Loyola University in Chicago and now a professor at the University of Massachusetts. Professor Zahn, the author of the challenging book, *German Catholics and Hitler's War,*[5] argues eloquently in an excellent brochure, *An Alternative to War,*[6] and in *War, Conscience and Dissent,*[7] that the only way for Christians to act in the present nuclear stalemate is to resort to the techniques of nonviolence. Professor Zahn summarizes his argument as follows:

> Since the quest for national security through violence has worked us into a corner where a resort to the means of violence now available to us would most likely provoke our own destruction and, with it, the destruction of a significant part of the world's population, the techniques of nonviolence being proposed as an alternative would present—assuming, of course, they were given the benefit of a degree of acceptance and official support comparable to that lavished upon the techniques of violence—the only reasonable hope for escape from that dilemma.[8]

Professor Zahn quite rightly insists that "we are dealing with something far more profound than a mere difference in policy options." He puts it this way:

> Our question ultimately concerns our basic conceptions of man. Is man, after all is said and done, a creature whose behavior is finally controlled through promises of physically satisfying rewards and threats of violently induced pain; or is he something greater, the deepest wellsprings of whose behavior contain forces responsive only to the power of love and recognition of common identity?[9]

Professor Zahn realistically concedes that the "mounting of a well-conceived and disciplined campaign of civil disobedience and noncooperation against an opponent using the means of violence might end with total victory for the latter."[10] But he suggests that since the destruction of millions of lives by America is the only possible alternative, then "it is better to perish as the victim of the inhumanity of others than to save oneself (or one's nation) by making others the victims of our own inhuman acts."[11]

The essence of Professor Zahn's difference with those Christians who feel that the United States should continue to have not a superiority, but a "sufficiency" of deterrent power, rests in Zahn's conception of human nature. It is his conviction that "even the totalitarian automaton will have to react as a man at some point,"[12] and consequently the "advocate of nonviolence is an optimist in that, trusting in the spiritual nature and destiny of man, he is confident that the capacity to love and to bear whatever sacrifices such love may entail is greater than the human capacity for evil. . . ."[13]

In *War, Conscience and Dissent* Zahn argues brilliantly that the longer the Free World subscribes to the philosophy of deterrence the "greater will grow the likelihood (one might almost say the certainty!) that one side or the other will strike the fatal spark and bring about the world-destroying exchange we are trying so hard to convine ourselves is impossible."[14]

Can anyone fathom the profound reasons why so very few Catholics in America follow the guidelines set forth so powerfully by the Catholic pacifist Gordon Zahn? Zahn himself furnishes one reason when he expresses his disappointment in the "frank unwillingness on the part of Church leaders to impose what may be regarded as too great a burden or impossible demands upon their faithful lest such excessive expectations cause a drop in active membership. . . ."[15] Mr. Zahn goes on to affirm that the Church "must itself be reconverted—or at least, reawakened—as to those value affirmations at least which, in its time of origin and its times of greatest glory, have always made it an institution for the transformation of society. ...."[16]

As I myself have read and reread Gordon Zahn's writings, I find my mind resisting his conclusions because, if I accept them, I must also believe that countless human beings and millions of Catholics have succumbed to nationalism and have compromised their faith to the point where they are willing to allow and even to participate in the massive violation of God's commandment, "Thou shalt not kill." In order to embrace Gordon Zahn's directives I must accept the proposition that the leaders and the faithful in the Catholic Church in America have been blinded over the past twenty-five years by the policies of public figures who have built a military empire ostensibly to preserve the safety of the American people, but which actually constitutes a system that requires American Christians each day to participate in the moral evil of threatening to inflict harm; this, when everyone knows that the infliction of such harm is inherently immoral.

At least one other American Catholic, James W. Douglass, sees the dilemma of the modern Christian as clearly as Gordon Zahn. He presents it in these words:

> One must either revolt against the disorder of the present system, for the sake of each man's right to the means of a human life, or cease being human oneself. The process of inhumanity and slow murder has already gone too far to allow an intermediate choice.[17]

Mr. Douglass' volume illustrates in a theological and mystical way the hideousness of the predicament in which America now finds itself. He points out, for example, that the total expenditure of the Peace Corps for an entire year is equal to the cost of thirty-two hours of the Vietnam war.

Mr. Douglass' treatment of the legal-moral issues of the nuclear age is arresting, but not always entirely clear or specific. He interweaves theology with the chronicle of contemporary events in such a manner that, though the language and the vision are intriguing, one is not entirely certain that a resolution of any problem is worked out at any particular level. He has, however, some magnificent statements on the problem of war such as the following:

> The roots of violence in man go far deeper than the just war doctrine and baptized nationalism characteristic of the Constantinian phase of Church history. In the history of man, the Church's involvement in violence has been merely a religious justification and extension of a prior human reality, the pervasive volence in mankind as a whole and its raging presence in each human heart.[18]

The "raging instinct in each human heart" towards violence has been described by Freud as the "death instinct." In Freud's famous public reply in 1933 to Albert Einstein's question to him, "Why does mankind wage war?" Freud stated that the underlying reason for war was the profound instinct in all human beings impelling them towards aggression and destruction. Freud consequently felt that there is no way to suppress the destructive tendencies of the death instinct within man, which has led mankind in almost every generation to the carnage of war, except by diverting these aggressive tendencies into channels other than that of warfare. Christian theologians would be inclined to state that man's instinct towards aggression and destruction is traceable to the sinfulness, and even inhumanity, which came to man after his fall from grace. Any explanation of war, however, or even of violence, must be articulated in more sophisticated and existential terms than the simple declaration that man, although redeemed, is still prone to violence because he is neither angel nor animal. The fact is that many acts of violence—and perhaps almost all wars—have been justified and rationalized throughout human history by eloquent if confused expressions of higher values, and even of the supreme value of love.

Is there than any middle ground between those who, like Gordon Zahn and James Douglass, opt for pacifism as the only Christian answer to the present arms race, and those who desire somehow to disarm gradually on a mutually agreeable basis and thus restore some semblance of rationality to the highly industrialized nations of the earth?

As much as I personally would like to claim that there is hope in working for disarmament, and all the other steps which would reverse the hysteria and irrationality which have dominated the twenty-five years of the nuclear age, I cannot see any significant promising signs or discover any probative evidence that such a reasonable solution is being worked out, or even can be worked out.

At the same time I and countless other millions have to be realistic and recognize that the mere suggestion of any unilateral weakening of the American defense posture is almost always greeted by the vast majority of Americans with scorn and ridicule. It may be that a significant number of young persons would be much more receptive to proposals that the United States take the initiative by some bold, daring, and even dangerous steps by which the arms race escalation could be reversed.

If one accepts the stark fact that the United States can contribute to peace only by some courageous, unilateral method of slowing the arms race then it follows that Catholics in America are involved in a collective silence which makes the silence of German Catholics in the decade of Hitler's atrocities almost insignificant by contrast. If, in other words, one comes to the conclusion that the situation is as desperate as Gordon Zahn and James Douglass relate, then one must accept the corollary that the one-fourth of the American nation who claim allegiance to the Catholic Church have acquiesced in nationalism or, even worse, in American capitalism, in a way which is a basis compromise with the unalterable principles of their religion.

Regardless, however, of one's own ultimate conviction with regard to the possible irreversibility of America's policy, everyone must work in some way to shock the mind and heart of America, which some twenty years ago adopted a policy of militaristic anticommunism that has now made it the most formidable bastion and fortress in the history of mankind. It is almost a great triumph even to raise a doubt in the average American's mind about the existing foreign policy of his country. To persuade him that his country made a tragic mistake, or committed a serious evil or sin twenty years ago, is almost impossible in most cases. Attempting to change the mind of any American adult who has subscribed to his nation's bipartisan foreign policy since the Truman Doctrine of 1948 is comparable to attempting to change the attitudes of a Southern segregationist towards integrated schools or of a white Northern racist toward interracial neighborhoods.

Theoretically it should be easier to alter the views of Catholics with respect to this question because of the rich Catholic tradition favoring the family of nations and urging the solidarity of all men throughout the world. The melancholy fact is, however, that it is probably more difficult to disabuse Catholics of their "hawkishness" against communism than it is other Americans. This phenomenon may be attributable to the rising socioeconomic status of Catholics; or to the almost paranoid fear of communism which entered into the psyche of Catholics as a result of the atrocities against the Catholic Church imputed to communism in the Mexican and Spanish revolutions, and in the Soviet take-over of Eastern Europe after the Second World War.

Without withdrawing my endorsement of the presentation of the starkness of America's moral dilemma as outlined by Gordon Zahn and James Douglass, I would like to suggest several intermediate or long-range proposals which, at the very least, may soften the abrasiveness in the Soviet-United States relationship. These proposals may, on the other hand, create some thawing of the feeling between the two armed camps that would lead to the withering away of their angry confrontation which has characterized the nuclear age.

Proposals aimed at this objective would include the following:

1. Reeducation of Young Americans

Clearly the reeducation of the young in America, with respect to the world they enter as adults, is imperative. It is almost self-evident that elementary and secondary education does not today prepare its students for the "One World" in which we now live. Edwin O. Reischauer, former U. S. ambassador to Japan, states this well in these words:

> Our elementary and secondary education, backed up by a lot of home conditioning, tends to convey a very misleading impression of the history of mankind, confirming false assumptions that the West is and has been superior to the other civilizations of mankind, and that its 19th century position of dominance over the rest of the world is natural and will continue indefinitely into the future. These are dangerous misconceptions for Americans to harbor in the second half of the 20th century.[19]

Reischauer insists that we would not tolerate the existence of a 19th century education in the natural sciences in contemporary American schools. He therefore maintains that we "should not tolerate in it the equally important field of the study of human civilization and the relations between nations."[20] He urges that all young American children be taught about the world as it is, describing it as follows:

> This is no longer a purely Western or even Western-dominated world. China and India are by far the most populous countries on the globe. Japan is a major economic and cultural force, showing promise of soon becoming the third most powerful nation in the world. It, as well as Pakistan, Indonesia, and Brazil overshadow in population the traditional great powers of Western Europe. The problems and wars that might blight our future are more likely to emerge from the unstable non-Western world than from the Occident.[21]

Is it visionary to think and to hope that Catholic schools in America might possess the tradition and the propensities for developing an imaginative and bold curriculum along the lines suggested by Professor Reischauer? Within the Catholic theological and philosophical tradition, as nowhere in Protestant or Jewish religious thought, there exists a body of truths and principles regarding the necessity, indispensability, and urgency of an international community made up of all nations linked together in the family of man and joined by the overarching principle of human equality and human solidarity.

Can the richness of this tradition be explored and exploited to the point where American Catholic elementary and secondary schools would be known as institutions in which students learn of the possibility and urgent necessity for an entirely new international order based on justice and motivated by brotherly love? At this particular time, when Catholic schools are seeking a new justification or raison d'etre, could they find this purpose in the pressing need in America for schools which will make their students fully aware of the problems and prospects of the peoples of Asia, Africa, and the Third World?

Difficulties involved in such a task are formidable. It is

questionable how many of the present personnel and pupil population of Catholic schools would have even a remote interest in changing the European-Christian orientation of their schools to a worldwide or global focus. Furthermore, public reaction to any school with a global orientation is likely to be adverse, and the opposition would come not merely from forces on the Right, but from the educational bureaucracy of the country. Such a shift in their focus would also seriously jeopardize any chances which Catholic schools might have at this time for further federal and state financial assistance for the secular aspects of their educational programs.

Catholic secondary schools could offer courses in Russian and Chinese, seminars in Buddhism, and offerings on all aspects of the problems of the Third World. Their freedom from the rigidities of the public school hierarchy would allow them to experiment in very significant ways with programs which could help a new generation of Americans to escape that myopia, excessive patriotism, and indifference to non-European cultures—all of which have combined to create and to perpetuate America's foreign policy of the last twenty years. This policy, in effect, has created a new Chinese wall —this time by nuclear warheads—in order to keep the "barbarians" far from our shores. Such a policy is likely to continue until the schools of America persuade a new generation that the West must understand the rich and diverse cultures and religions of the non-Western peoples, who outnumber Occidentals by close to 3 to 1.

It is difficult to think of a challenge to Catholic schools in America that is more important or pressing than the need to develop a curriculum which would begin to prepare them to live as citizens and as Christians in a world whose under-developed nations will not long tolerate the squandering of mankind's resources to their detriment and deprivation in the Soviet-American impasse.

2. Reduction in the International Sales of American Weapons

A second area for promising reform is existing American policy with regard to the furnishing of arms to foreign powers. In 1968 the United States spent $79.3 billion for military purposes while the Soviet Union spent $35.8 billion. For the United States this meant some 10 percent of its national income in that year.

During 1968 the United States was the largest supplier of weapons to the nations of the world. The total came to nearly $719 million including sales, grants, and training. Both the Soviet Union and the United States gave military aid to the Middle East before and during 1968. The Middle East showed the sharpest rise in military spending, increasing by nearly 20 percent annually over the last three years. Arms spending by developing nations has also been rising, usually at the annual rate of about 7.5 percent, although national production of nonmilitary items has been increasing in those countries by about 5 percent and often a good deal less.

The commercial motivation and the industrial empires behind the distribution by the United States of all types of military weapons to all types of nations around the globe has been exposed in such books as *The War Business: The International Trade in Armaments* by George Thayer.* As never before, Mr. Thayer has demonstrated that the United States is ultimately responsible for allowing the introduction of unneeded and unmanageable sophisticated weapon systems, such as jet fighters, tanks, and submarines, into relatively tranquil locales in Latin America. Thus America has permitted the creation of mini-arms races between poverty-stricken nations which have little or no basis for conflict.

On a related problem, John Kennedy Galbraith, in his

*New York: Simon and Schuster, Inc., 1969.

volume, *How to Control the Military,* * revealed that nearly seven hundred retired generals, admirals, and navy captains are employed by the ten largest defense contractors, thus intensifying the complex linkage between the manufacturers of arms and the Pentagon itself. Equally chilling is the revelation of Richard J. Barnet in his volume, *The Economy of Death.* ** In a Kafka-like story the author shows how the public has been consistently shortchanged by irrational and wasteful decisions, as, for example, the expenditure of more than $23 billion worth of missiles that were never deployed.

Is there any way by which the facts revealed in these volumes can somehow become operative in American public policy? The ordinary person, even if he never questions the need for some kind of defense system, feels voiceless and powerless in confrontation with the public policy—indeed, a private-public conspiracy—by which the United States continues to merchandise the weapons of war to the entire world, and thereby makes war more probable. Papal statements have been frequent and eloquent in condemning the introduction of armaments into nations which very often can ill-afford to spend their limited resources on this type of product. American commentators of every sort have frequently pointed out that the United States, in allowing corporations to create and then satisfy the desire for weapons in foreign nations, is in effect promoting a military solution to complex social problems.

Is there any way by which the highly organized units of the Catholic Church in America can initiate and coordinate a national campaign to turn American policy around, at least insofar as the merchandising of arms to other nations is concerned? The monthly *Catholic Worker,* the *Catholic Peace Fellowship,* and similar groups certainly advocate the diminution of the sale of American weapons to foreign nations;

*New York: Doubleday & Company, Inc., 1969.
**New York: Atheneum Publishers, 1969.

but these peace groups have never been near the mainstream of American Catholic activity. On the question of the severe control of such sales, however, could there not be a Catholic consensus which would make its voice heard, much like the crusade mounted by Congressman Richard D. McCarthy on chemical-biological warfare, which led, in November 1969, to President Nixon banning those forms of warfare, at least in a defensive war?

One wonders whether it is possible to arouse the indignation of American Catholics concerning any one of the outrages which now go on in the name of America's foreign policy. Over the past generation they have been united and emboldened to speak out on issues related to discrimination against Catholics running for public office, practices denying aid to Catholic schools, and laws designed to ease abortion statutes. If it is possible at all to have any area of consensus among Catholics on the overall issue of peace and war, it would appear that such a consensus might and could happen with regard to the dismaying fact that American munition makers are the merchants of death throughout the world.

3. Unilateral Disarmament

For all Christians who are unable or unwilling to accept the proposals of the pure pacifists, the third fruitful area for exploration is bilateral disarmament. The record, to be sure, is not encouraging. Starting in 1946 with the meetings of the United Nations Atomic Energy Commission, which spent several months considering the Baruch version of the Acheson-Lilienthal proposal for the control of atomic energy, there has been a long series of meetings between the delegates of the Eastern and Western powers in various attempts to arrest the arms race. In 1952 the United Nations Disarmament Commission initiated a series of meetings which proved to be almost fruitless. In 1954 and 1955 the same commission held a series of somewhat more productive meetings in London. The record of such meetings, including the Geneva conferences, have produced libraries of books and learned articles but few results in the diminution of the actual amount of military hardware in the possession of the major powers.

The case for unilateral disarmament has been made effectively by Erich Fromm in the volume *Arms Control, Disarmament and National Security*[22] In reading his essay, in conjunction with the twenty-two essays in this volume, one is struck by the fact that there appear to be so many psychological inhibitions towards any disarmament on the part of both the Soviet Union and the United States that, ultimately, if the nuclear stalemate is ever to be broken, it may have to be through some form of limited unilateral disarmament by either country. Fromm, a professor of psychoanalysis at Michigan State University, compares the American dogma that "the Russians cannot be trusted" to a paranoiac's unshakable conviction in the validity of a delusion simply because the delusion is logically possible. Americans have come to think, in other words, that since a Russian attack is possible, it is therefore certain, unless we resist it at every moment. Fromm points out that, without indulging in irresponsible antimilitarism, America as a nation must learn that the only sane and realistic way of conducting the affairs of individual, as well as national life, is to deal with probabilities and not mere possibilities.

Those who find Erich Fromm's position unconvincing should at least give the most serious consideration to a more limited concept of unilateral disarmament, such as the position which has been called by Charles Osgood "graduated unilateral action or disengagement." In his well-known article on this subject,[23] Mr. Osgood suggests that an act of unilateral disarmament should be clearly disadvantageous to the side making it and should be able to be so perceived by the enemy, who recognizes that the external threat to his existence has been reduced. Furthermore, the unilateral act of disarmament should, according to Osgood, be of such a nature that reciprocal action by the enemy may be tactfully taken, since the initiator's act has been made in full view of the entire world in a way which cannot be construed as a mere trick.

Actions consistent with Mr. Osgood's position would, for example, be decisions to share scientific information, to reduce the number of troops outside the continental United States, to evacuate one or more military bases, and to admit Red China to the United Nations.

Despite the clear desirability of having some type of disarmament, however acquired, the gloomy fact remains that disarmament, even for the diplomats professionally involved in it, is an unending series of difficult and seemingly unanswerable questions. Outside observers to the disarmament conferences conducted over the past several years face the further difficulty of seeking needles of serious discussion in haystacks of propaganda. In September 1959, for example, Soviet Premier Khrushchev appeared before the United Nations General Assembly and proposed "general and complete disarmament." Although the West regarded this proposal as a hypocritical travesty on history and logic, Western diplomats, not desiring to be maneuvered into a position of seeming bellicosity before world opinion, turned up with their own disarmament plan. Discussions, which were mostly denunciations, lingered on in a maze of unrealism until June 27, 1960, when all negotiations were terminated.

The frustrations felt by both parties to this conference, so often duplicated in similar conferences during the twenty-five years of the nuclear age, resulted in large part from the constant fear of both the Soviet Union and the United States of being assaulted and pulverized by the opponent. This mutual fear is perceptively described by Herman Kahn who, as a strategic analyst and military planner with the Rand Corporation, is not a proponent of unilateral disarmament. Kahn writes that

> Aside from the ideological differences and the problem of security itself, there does not seem to be any objective quarrel between the United States and Russia that justifies the risks and costs that we subject each other to. The big thing that the Soviet Union and the United States have to fear from each other is fear itself.[24]

This fear is widely articulated in the United States to mean that the Soviet Union is out to conquer the world for communism and that, if the United States disarmed even in a limited way, Russia would be all the more eager to accomplish her desire for world domination. Although those most learned in Soviet intentions, and in the theory and application of Marxism, state that the alleged desire of Russia for world domination is an erroneous interpretation of the nature of the present-day Soviet Union, it would seem to be almost impossible to convince any significant number of individuals in America that the Russian revolution, as designed by Lenin and Trotsky, is no longer operative. Hardly anyone in America, aside from the specialists, recognizes that the victory of Stalin and the annihilation of almost all the old Bolsheviks brought about a radical change in the nature of Soviet communism. The system which Stalin built was neither socialist nor revolutionary but, rather, a form of state capitalism based upon authoritarian methods of planning and economic centralization.

Once again very few Americans realize that Khrushchev did not change the basic character of Soviet society. He did not make it a revolutionary or even a socialist regime but one of the more conservative and even class-ridden regimes in the Western world. It is therefore a pernicious oversimplification to try to explain Khrushchev by quoting Marx, Lenin, or Trotsky, and thereby deducing that the dominant ambition of the Soviet Union is to conquer all capitalist and under-developed nations as soon as feasible. Such a notion, so widely held in the United States, demonstrates not only a total failure to understand the historical development which has taken place in Russia, but also an inability or incapacity to appreciate the enormous difference between facts and ideologies.

American fears and phobias regarding the intentions imputed to Communists over the past generation have made every public official, appointed or elected, at every level of government, avoid any view which might earn him the description of being "soft" on communism. Since this charge would be made against the proponent of even the most insignificant unilateral steps towards disarmament, we must realistically admit that any advocacy of new alternatives in this area cannot reasonably be expected to come from governmental authority; therefore the burden and the pressing duty to shatter the idol of anticommunism in America must come from Christians and others who are persuaded that the only possible way of ending the risk of horrifying war rests in a form of unilateral action by the United States. It may be that such action, by rejecting the hatred of communism so dominant over the last generation, will affirm the great spiritual values of democracy in such a way that the Communists, and all peoples of the earth, will experience an abatement of that fear of extinction which has so shriveled the consciences of Americans and all others involved in the nuclear stalemate of the Cold War.

There is some indication that the American mind is ambivalent or divided with respect to the advisability of continuing the bipartisan foreign policy of the past generation. It is significant, as Eugene V. Rostow notes in his book, *Law, Power and the Pursuit of Peace,* that "President Truman and President Johnson were destroyed politically by Korea and Vietnam."[25] Hopefully there is a slowly rising tide of opinion in the United States that would openly concede that the Soviet Union and America are like scorpions in a bottle which cannot move without inflicting massive damage on each other. At the same time there is a persistently held view that the best thing that the United States can now achieve is some type of stabilization of the balance of terror. What is clearly needed is a determination on the part of the American public and the United States government to achieve major reductions in nuclear forces and ultimately to secure their elimination under a system of effective international control. Since the first deliberations on the Baruch Plan almost twenty-five years ago, the terrible contest in superfluous strategic weapons between Russia and the United States has taken on the aura of an international game in which the stakes are beyond human imagination. But the very concept of a "game" promotes the further concept that a gain for one side is inevitably a loss for the other. The game is senseless, however, because both sides lose by "winning," and neither side can win except by stopping the "game."

For Christians and humanists who believe in the inviolability and sanctity of every human life, the imperious call to disarmament is a summons to subdue those fears that have made prisoners and cowards of the millions of people who are victims of the illusions and delusions of the nuclear era.

4. Creation of New Political Directions

Those who are not entirely persuaded that unilateral disarmament is the one way to bring peace may work towards the prevention of war by the creation of a new political party in America or by the "capture" of an existing national political party. Any suggestion that Christians—and especially Catholics—who are interested in peace should form a new political party immediately brings united and hostile reactions, accompanied by adverse reports about the history and activities of Church-affiliated political parties in Europe.

The emergence of a political party devoted to peace is, however, inevitable in the United States. Therefore the only question is the extent to which Christians will fashion and formulate the positions and the platform of the political party that will be born of America's revulsion at the foreign policy which has brought about a nuclear nightmare, genocide in Asia, and a scandalous situation in which the richest nation on earth becomes richer while hunger and illiteracy grow among more than one-half of humanity.

One of the most serious obstacles to the formation of a political movement seeking a radical change in America's foreign policy is the hope or illusion that somehow things will work out so that a new party will not be necessary. Indeed, amidst the agonies of protest against the Vietnam war, few if any of the militants look to the larger issues of America's stance in the world after the Vietnam holocaust.

In the emergence of a movement for an entirely new foreign policy, a second serious difficulty is the real impossibility for most American citizens to acquire accurate knowledge about the actual implementation of America's foreign policy. A series of events related by Henry A. Kissinger in his book, *American Foreign Policy: Three Essays,* [26] illustrate the point. Mr. Kissinger, prior to his becoming a close adviser to President Nixon on foreign policy, wrote the following:

> The sequence of events that led to negotiations [in Vietnam] probably started with General Westmoreland's visit to Washington in November 1967. On that occasion, General Westmoreland told a joint session of Congress that the war was being militarily won. He outlined "indicators" of progress and stated that a limited withdrawal of United States combat forces might be undertaken beginning late in 1968. On January 17, 1968, President Johnson, in his State of the Union address, emphasized that the pacification program—the extension of the control of Saigon into the countryside—was

progressing satisfactorily. Sixty-seven percent of the population of Vietnam lived in relatively secure areas; the figure was
expected to rise. A week later, the Tet offensive overthrew the
assumptions of American strategy."[27]

This incident is a dramatic illustration of the serious loss of
credibility which the United States government has now sus-
tained with its people. Almost countless other incidents in
which the United States has misstated the facts about its
operations in a foreign country could be cited. One, that
affected me and the other seven members of the U. S. Study
Team on Political and Religious Freedom in South Vietnam,
occurred in the White House itself in May 1969. On that
occasion a highly placed official of the National Security
Council assured some members of the Study Team that the
number of political prisoners in South Vietnam had certainly
gone down and that the number of such individuals was no
longer a problem. The embassy in Saigon, however,
conceded after rigorous cross-examination that the number
of political prisoners in South Vietnam had in fact gone up
over the past several months—due in large part to the activities of the U. S. Pacification Program!

Americans who are determined to take appropriate political action to bring about a radical change in the foreign
policy of their nation face an almost insurmountable obstacle
in the impossibility of acquiring accurate information from
their own government with regard to what this nation's personnel are doing in foreign lands. The clandestine political
activities of the CIA constitute a further barrier to the people
having real knowledge of how its government functions in
the world. As Edwin O. Reischauer says in *Beyond Vietnam*,
the covert activities of the CIA "are a net loss to us abroad,
and running counter as they do to our own concepts of morality, they probably do even more serious internal injury to us
at home."[28]

American Christians who aspire to mount an offensive

against a government that has sought to keep the truth from its people, and even, on occasion, to deceive them, face a task of immense difficulty. As Christians they must follow the piercing insights in a volume entitled *The Politics of the Gospel* by Jean Marie Paupert.* This French lay theologian shows that Christianity is an utterly incarnational religion and, consequently, politics must be coextensive with life. For Paupert—and perhaps for all totally convinced Christians— the teaching of the Gospel must in some sense be both entirely religious and entirely political. Although Paupert has succeeded in elucidating an explicit political teaching from his exegesis of the scriptural text, he does not elaborate on the application of these principles to the reformation of a government which has become militaristic.

The difficulties facing those who would try to work out a new foreign policy for America by political means will almost certainly increase rather than decrease. Militarism on the one hand moves forward with a vigorous self-pollination, utilizing the appeals of communism, national defense, and patriotism, all put together in an amalgam somewhat like a religion, as the basis on which the defense establishment can justify its existence and its expansion. On the other hand the world after Vietnam will almost inevitably bring about some form of neoisolationism in America. If the Viet Cong succeed in taking over South Vietnam, the voices of anticommunism will plead that now the Communists are a thousand miles nearer to the United States than before and that consequently we must rearm even more extensively. Those Americans who desire a completely new foreign policy will conclude from the Vietnam experience that any intervention in a guerrilla war in an underdeveloped nation does not make sense for America and that as a result the United States should retreat to a position of relative isolationism in the world.

Once again, Catholics, by reason of their fruitful theologi-

*New York: Holt, Rinehart & Winston, Inc., 1969.

cal and philosophical tradition, should theoretically be in a better position to develop the mystique and ideology for a political movement which would be based on the concept that America has a role to make possible the good life for all of humanity. The Catholic tradition has rejected views such as those of Hobbes and Locke. The Catholic viewpoint of the state has refused to accept the individualistic social contract theory, which seeks to restrict the role of a state to the minimal function of preventing the more violent acts of men who are deemed to be essentially asocial. The political ideal accepted by Catholic tradition goes back to the Greeks, and teaches that the purpose of society is to fulfill man's nature within a community, to make possible for him the good life, and to assist him to realize his highest intellectual and spiritual potentialities.

American political theory has generally embraced an unsettled combination of both these competing moral and political philosophies. An uneasy alliance of these two objectives runs, for example, throughout the ideologies present in the American public school. Within the next few years America must make some decision as to which of these contending philosophies it will choose with regard to its role in the world. All but the most fervid nationalists must admit that the rich nations of the earth, like America, have an obligation to the poor nations, just as the wealthy states of the United States have an obligation to the poorer ones. The crucial question will be the extent to which the American social contract contains more than the Hobbes-Lockean imperatives of the minimal protection of life, liberty, and property. Those who feel that America cannot limit itself to this lowest attainable goal must come to some agreement as to the content and extent of America's commitment to a common enterprise, whose aim is a better life both for the citizens of the United States and for all mankind.

Americans who reject the notion that the United States can

protect itself and other nations in the Free World by a policy of massive militarism must determine the extent to which this country can be or should be "messianic." In the formation of this nation, America certainly spoke in "messianic" terms. The nation stated in the Declaration of Independence that *all* men are created equal and endowed with certain rights. During the early days of American history there was the constant proclamation that the era of kings was over and that American independence was the first blow in a world revolution for freedom and prosperity.

For those who desire a radically new foreign policy, the ultimate question is whether the basic social contract which binds Americans together has always had implicit within it a world mission as one of its components. This world mission, or idealism, is apparent in Woodrow Wilson's Fourteen Points and in Franklin Roosevelt's Four Freedoms. A century ago it was adumbrated by Abraham Lincoln in these words:

> I have often inquired of myself, what great principle or idea it was that kept this Confederacy so long together. It was not the mere matter of the separation of the colonies from the motherland; but something in that Declaration giving liberty, not alone of the people of this country, but hope to the world for all future time. It was that which gave promise that in due time the weight should be lifted from the shoulders of all men, and that all should have an equal chance. This is the sentiment embodied in that Declaration of Independence. . . .

In the world after the Vietnam war, the 6 percent of humanity who live in the United States will, as never before, be scrutinized by the 94 percent of humanity, or more than three billion people, whose lives and destinies will be affected in countless ways by the policies which the United States adopts. Catholics constitute about one-fourth of that 6 percent living in the nation whose public decisions within the next few years can produce or prevent political anarchy and economic collapse around the globe.

It seems self-evident, then, that American Catholics have before them an opportunity of surpassing importance and urgency—perhaps the most significant opportunity which they have ever had in the history of the United States. If Catholics, aided by many others, can define and refine the wealth of their theological and political traditions, and articulate and act upon them in sociopolitical ways, they may be able to persuade the nation that it has a moral commitment to mankind which it should observe, not only because it is useful to America, but—more importantly—because it is right.

Notes

1. *The Church and War—A Catholic Study* (New York: Sheed and Ward, 1928).

2. "To Cap the Volcano," *Foreign Affairs* (October 1969), p. 9.

3. *Ibid.*, p. 11.

4. *Ibid.*

5. (New York: Sheed and Ward, 1962).

6. (New York: Council on Religion and International Affairs, 1963).

7. (New York: Hawthorn Books, Inc., 1967).

8. *An Alternative to War*, pp. 22-23.

9. *Ibid.*, p. 31.

10. *Ibid.*, p. 14.

11. *Ibid.*, pp. 14-15.

12. *Ibid.*, p. 14.

13. *Ibid.*, p. 15.

14. *War, Conscience and Dissent.*

15. *An Alternative to War*, p. 27.

16. *Ibid.*

17. *The Non-Violent Cross: A Theology of Revolution and Peace* (New York: The Macmillan Company, 1968), p. 8.

18. *Ibid.*, p. 218.

19. *Beyond Vietnam: The United States and Asia* (New York: Random House, Inc., 1967), p. 235.

20. *Ibid.*, p. 242.

21. *Ibid.*

22. Donald G. Brennan, ed. (New York: George Braziller, Inc., 1961).

23. *Bulletin of Atomic Scientists* (1960).
24. *Stanford Research Institute Journal* (1959).
25. (Lincoln: University of Nebraska Press, 1968).
26. (New York: W. W. Norton & Company, Inc., 1969).
27. *Ibid.,* p. 101.
28. Reischauer, *op. cit.,* p. 221.

A.

Annotated Bibliography of Selected Books
on Christian Attitudes to War

THE FOLLOWING is an annotated bibliography of the all-too-few
volumes written from a Christian point of view on the morality of
war. No attempt has been made to compile a bibliography of peri-
odical literature, the best of which is listed in some of the volumes
noted below.

Bainton, Roland H. *Christian Attitudes toward War and Peace. A
    Historical Survey and Critical Re-evaluation.* Nashville, Tenn.:
    Abingdon Press, 1960. This survey of Christian attitudes to-
    ward war is possibly the best one-volume summary of the view-
    points of all denominations in Christian history. Professor
    Bainton, of the Yale University Divinity School, tends to be a
    pacifist, but presents a well-informed and very readable chroni-
    cle of Christian reactions through the past twenty centuries
    towards the phenomenon of warfare.
Bennett, John C., Ed. *Nuclear Weapons and the Conflict of Con-*

science. New York: Charles Scribner's Sons, 1962.

This collection of seven essays by Protestant writers ranges from a plea for unilateral disarmament by Erich Fromm to the advocacy of the possibility of a just war by Paul Ramsey. An excellent essay by Dr. John C. Bennett, along with other contributions, makes this volume a notable and valuable exploration of the issues from a non-Catholic, Christian point of view.

Douglass, James W. *The Non-Violent Cross—A Theology of Revolution and Peace.* New York: The Macmillan Co., 1968.

It is the contention of Douglass in this volume that the primary task of today's Christian theologian is to open the way towards a transformation of mankind through nonviolent means. Douglass attempts to provide a basis for a nonviolent revolution established upon the theories of Gandhi, the secular death-of-God theologies, and Marxist doctrine. The volume is clearly one of the most provocative written by any contemporary Catholic writer.

Flannery, Harry W., Ed. *Pattern for Peace—Catholic Statements on International Order.* Westminster, Md.: The Newman Press, 1962.

This is a valuable collection of all the significant statements made by Roman pontiffs, from Leo XIII through John XXIII. The document also includes statements on peace and war by the Catholic bishops of America from 1941 to 1960.

Lawler, Justus George. *Nuclear War: The Ethic, the Rhetoric, the Reality, a Catholic Assessment.* Westminster, Md.: The Newman Press, 1966.

This evaluation of nuclear war, by the founder and editor of the quarterly *Continuum,* is written with a combination of fact and feeling which will appeal to many readers. It is one of the better reasoned attempts by Catholic thinkers to find some way out of the maze of contradictions in an age when any war may become global.

Marty, Martin E., and Peerman, Dean G., Eds. *New Theology No. 6.* New York: The Macmillan Co., 1969.

This gathering together of seventeen essays on theology and revolution is an uneven but important document that contains insights not available elsewhere about radical movements in the

Third World. Of particular importance is the reproduction in the book of the manifesto issued in 1966 by sixteen bishops of the Third World. Entitled "The Gospel and Revolution," this remarkable document was authored by bishops from Algeria, Brazil, Colombia, Egypt, Yugoslavia, Lebanon, China, and Laos.

Merton, Thomas, Ed. *Breakthrough to Peace: Twelve Views on the Threat of Thermonuclear Extermination.* New York: New Directions, 1962.

This collection represents the most forceful presentation of a nuclear pacifist position by Catholics. It is similar to, and supports, a series of essays by British Roman Catholic scholars, edited by Walter Stein and published in London under the title *Nuclear Weapons and Christian Conscience* (London: Merlin Press, 1961), and later in the United States as *Nuclear Weapons: A Catholic Response* (New York: Sheed and Ward, 1962). Another work in this vein, edited by Charles S. Thompson, is *Morals and Missiles: Catholic Essays on the Problem of War Today* (London: James Clark, 1959).

Nagle, William J., Ed. *Morality and Modern Warfare.* Baltimore, Md.: Helicon Press, Inc., 1960.

This collection of ten essays by American Catholics is one of the best anthologies in the sparse literature by Catholics about modern and nuclear warfare. It contains articles by John Courtney Murray, S. J.; John C. Ford, S.J.; Prof. Gordon C. Zahn, and William V. O'Brien. A fifteen-page bibliography, though somewhat outdated, contains a comprehensive list of books and articles written from a Christian viewpoint on the problem of war.

Nuttal, Geoffrey F. *Christian Pacifism and History.* Oxford, England: Basil Blackwell, 1958.

Nuttal's study is possibly the best of the many studies on pacifism, not all of which are easy to locate. Reference to pacifist sources are not ordinarily noted in standard works on international law, political philosophy, or Christian theology. William Robert Miller has compiled a *Bibliography of Books on War, Pacifism, Non-Violence and Related Studies,* which was published by the Fellowship of Reconciliation in 1961.

O'Brien, William V. *War and/or Survival.* New York: Doubleday & Company, 1969. In this book Dr. O'Brien, chairman of the

Institute of World Polity at Georgetown University, presents a well-informed and well-reasoned case for the application of traditional Catholic moral principles to war, including nuclear warfare. This volume, along with the author's book, *Nuclear War, Deterrence and Morality* (Westminster, Md.: The Newman Press, 1967), makes Dr. O'Brien one of the most articulate and prolific spokesmen on behalf of the adequacy and relevancy of traditional Catholic teaching with respect to armed conflict between nations.

Potter, Ralph B. *War and Moral Discourse.* Richmond Va.: John Knox Press, 1969. One of the most valuable features of this paperback book, by a professor at the Harvard Divinity School, is its forty-page bibliographical essay in which all the major contemporary studies on the morality of war are evaluated. Towards the end of this essay Professor Potter warns that a "great deal of what is published is of very mediocre quality." He therefore suggests that persons concerned about the morality of war "might better use their time reading basic materials, such as Roland Bainton's volume, and doing some hard thinking on their own."

Ramsey, Paul. *The Just War—Force and Political Responsibility.* New York: Charles Scribner's Sons, 1968.

In this 550-page volume Professor Ramsey, of Princeton Theological Seminary, synthesizes in twenty-four chapters the reasons why he endorses, to a large extent, the traditional Christian viewpoint with regard to a just war. The book is without doubt the *locus classicus* for the argumentation of those who seek to find a rationale for modern war within the framework and terminology of traditional ethical and moral teaching.

Tucker, Robert W. *The Just War—A Study in Contemporary American Doctrine.* Baltimore, Md.: The Johns Hopkins Press, 1960.

While this sophisticated study is not written from a specifically Christian point of view, it is a profound study of the moral implications of American attitudes towards the possibility of a just war and the ethical options available at this time to the United States.

Zahn, Gordon C. *War, Conscience and Dissent.* New York: Hawthorn Books, Inc., 1967.

In this volume Zahn rejects the notion that the criteria of the just war doctrine should be the guidelines for determining the moral permissibility of Christian participation in war in the modern world. He goads and challenges the defenders of the just war theory to observe these criteria in actual practice. The practical ineffectiveness of these criteria, as restraints upon conduct in war, is one of the main theses of this important book.

Reprinted from the *Catholic Mind* (October 1963).

B.

Excerpts on Peace and War from
Pacem in Terris (Peace on Earth),
encyclical of Pope John XXIII issued
in April, 1963

DISARMAMENT

109. On the other hand, it is with deep sorrow that We note the enormous stocks of armaments that have been and still are being made in the more economically developed countries with a vast outlay of intellectual and economic resources. And so it happens that, while the people of these countries are loaded with heavy burdens, other countries as a result are deprived of the collaboration they need in order to make economic and social progress.

110. The production of arms is allegedly justified on the grounds that in present-day conditions peace cannot be preserved without an equal balance of armaments. And so, if one country increases its armaments, others feel the need to do the same. And if one country is equipped with nuclear weapons, other countries must produce their own, equally destructive.

111. Consequently, people live in constant fear lest the storm that threatens every moment should break upon them with dreadful violence. And with good reason, for the arms of war are ready at hand. Even though it is difficult to believe that anyone would deliberately take the responsibility for the appalling destruction and sorrow that war would bring in its train, it cannot be denied that the conflagration may be set off by some uncontrollable and unexpected chance. And one must bear in mind that, even though the monstrous power of modern weapons acts as a deterrent, it is to be feared that the mere continuance of nuclear tests, undertaken with war in mind, will have fatal consequences for life on earth.

112. Justice, right reason and humanity, therefore, urgently demand that the arms race should cease; that the stockpiles which exist in various countries should be reduced equally and simultaneously by the parties concerned; that nuclear weapons should be banned; and that a general agreement should eventually be reached about progressive disarmament and an effective method of control.

In the words of Pius XII, Our predecessor of happy memory: *The calamity of a world war, with the economic and social ruin and the moral excesses and dissolution that accompany it, must not be permitted to envelop the human race for a third time.*[59]

113. All must realize that there is no hope of putting an end to the building up of armaments, nor of reducing the present stocks, nor still less of abolishing them altogether, unless the process is complete and thorough and unless it proceeds from inner conviction; unless, that is, everyone sincerely co-operates to banish the fear and anxious expectation of war with which men are oppressed. If this is to come about, the fundamental principle on which our present peace depends must be replaced by another, which declares that the true and solid peace of nations can consist, not in equality of arms, but in mutual trust alone.

We believe that this can be brought to pass, and We consider that it is something which reason requires, that it is eminently desirable in itself and that it will prove to be the source of many benefits.

114. In the first place, it is an objective demanded by reason. There can be, or at least there should be, no doubt that relations

between states, as between individuals, should be regulated, not by the force of arms, but by the light of reason, by the rule, that is, of truth, of justice and of active and sincere co-operation.

115. Secondly, We say that it is an objective earnestly to be desired in itself. Is there anyone who does not ardently yearn to see war banished, to see peace preserved and daily more firmly established?

116. And finally, it is an objective which will be a fruitful source of many benefits, for its advantages will be felt everywhere—by individuals, by families, by nations, by the whole human family. The warning of Pius XII still rings in our ears: *Nothing is lost by peace; everything may be lost by war.*[60]

117. Since this is so, We, the Vicar on earth of Jesus Christ, Saviour of the world and author of peace, as interpreter of the profound longing of the entire human family, following the paternal impulse of Our heart and seized by anxiety for the good of all, feel it Our duty to beseech men, especially those who have the responsibility of public affairs, to spare no labor in order to insure that world events follow a reasonable and human course.

118. In the highest and most authoritative assemblies, let men give serious thought to the problem of a peaceful adjustment of relations between political communities on a world level—an adjustment founded on mutual trust, on sincerity in negotiations and on faithful fulfillment of obligations assumed. Let them study the problems until they find that point of agreement from which they can commence to go forward toward accords that will be sincere, lasting and fruitful.

119. We, for Our part, will not cease to pray God to bless these labors so that they may lead to fruitful results.

In Freedom

120. It has also to be borne in mind that relations between states should be based on freedom. This is to say that no country may unjustly oppress others or unduly meddle in their affairs. On the contrary, all should help to develop in others a sense of responsibility, a spirit of enterprise and an earnest desire to be the first to promote their own advancement.

EVOLUTION OF UNDERDEVELOPED COUNTRIES

121. Because all men are joined together by reason of their common origin, their redemption by Christ and their supernatural destiny, and are called to form one Christian family, We appealed in the encyclical *Mater et Magistra* to economically developed nations to come to the aid of those which are in the process of development.[61]

122. We are greatly consoled to see how widely that appeal has been favorably received. And We are confident that even more so in the future it will contribute to the end that the poorer countries, in as short a time as possible, will arrive at that degree of economic development which will enable every citizen to live in keeping with his human dignity.

123. But it can never be sufficiently repeated that this co-operation should be effected with the greatest respect for the liberty of the countries being developed, for these must realize that they are primarily responsible, and that they are the principal artisans in the promotion of their own economic development and social progress.

124. Our predecessor Pius XII wisely proclaimed that *in the matter of this new order founded on moral principles, there is no room for violation of freedom, integrity and security of other nations, no matter what may be their territorial extent or their capacity for defense. It is inevitable that the powerful states, by reason of their greater potential and their power, should pave the way in the establishment of economic groups comprising not only themselves but also smaller and weaker states as well. It is nevertheless indispensable that in the interests of the common good they, as all others, should respect the rights of those smaller states to political freedom, to economic development and to the adequate protection, in the case of conflicts between nations, of that neutrality which is theirs according to the natural, as well as international, law. Those states likewise have the right to safeguard their economic development. In this way, and in this way only, will they be able to obtain a fitting share of the common good, and assure the material and spiritual welfare of their people.*[62]

125. It is vitally important, therefore, that the wealthier states, in providing varied forms of assistance to the poorer, should respect the moral heritage and ethnic characteristics peculiar to each, and

also that they should avoid any intention of political domination. If this is done, *a precious contribution will be made toward the formation of a world community, a community in which each member, while conscious of its own individual rights and duties, will work in a relationship of equality toward the attainment of the universal common good.*[63]

Signs of the Times

126. Men are becoming more and more convinced that disputes which arise between states should not be resolved by recourse to arms, but rather by negotiation.

127. It is true that on historical grounds this conviction is based chiefly on the terrible destructive force of modern arms. And it is nourished by the horror aroused in the mind by the very thought of the cruel destruction and the immense suffering which the use of those armaments would bring. And for this reason it is hardly possible to imagine that in the atomic era war could be used as an instrument of justice.

128. Nevertheless, unfortunately, the law of fear still reigns among peoples, and it forces them to spend fabulous sums for armaments: not for aggression, they affirm—and there is no reason for not believing them—but to dissuade others from aggression.

129. There is reason to hope, however, that by meeting and negotiating men may come to discover better the bonds—deriving from the human nature which they have in common—that unite them, and that they may learn also that one of the most profound requirements of their common nature is this: that between them and their respective peoples it is not fear that should reign, but love, a love that tends to express itself in a collaboration that is loyal, manifold in form and productive of many benefits.

INTERDEPENDENCE BETWEEN POLITICAL COMMUNITIES

130. Recent progress in science and technology has profoundly affected human beings and influenced men to work together and live as one family. There has been a great increase in the circulation of ideas, of persons and of goods from one country to another, so that relations have become closer between individuals, families and in-

termediate associations belonging to different political communities, and between the public authorities of those communities.

131. At the same time the interdependence of national economies has grown deeper, one becoming progressively more closely related to the other, so that they become, as it were, integral parts of the one world economy. Likewise the social progress, order, security and peace of each country are necessarily connected with the social progress, order, security and peace of all other countries.

132. At the present time no political community is able to pursue its own interests and develop itself in isolation, because the degree of its prosperity and development is a reflection and a component part of the degree of prosperity and development of all the other political communities.

INSUFFICIENCY OF MODERN STATES
TO ENSURE THE UNIVERSAL COMMON GOOD

133. The unity of the human family has always existed because its members were human beings all equal by virtue of their natural dignity. Hence there will always exist the objective need to promote in sufficient measure the universal common good, that is the common good of the entire human family.

134. In times past, one could be justified in feeling that the public authorities of the different political communities might be in a position to provide for the universal common good either through normal diplomatic channels or top-level meetings, or by making use of juridical instruments such as conventions and treaties, for example juridical instruments suggested by the natural law and regulated by the law of nations and international law.

As a result of the far-reaching changes which have taken place in the relations of the human family, the universal common good gives rise to problems which are complex, very grave and extremely urgent, especially as regards security and world peace. On the other hand, the public authorities of the individual political communities —placed as they are on a footing of equality one with the other— no matter how much they multiply their meetings or sharpen their wits in efforts to draw up new juridical instruments, they are no longer capable of facing the task of finding an adequate solution to

the problems mentioned above. And this not due to a lack of good
will or of a spirit of enterprise, but because of a structural defect
which hinders them.

135. It can be said, therefore, that at this historical moment the
present system of organization and the way its principle of authority
operates on a world basis no longer correspond to the objective
requirements of the universal common good.

CONNECTION BETWEEN THE COMMON GOOD
AND POLITICAL AUTHORITY

136. There exists an intrinsic connection between the common
good on the one hand and the structure and function of public
authority on the other. The moral order, which needs public authority in order to promote the common good in human society, requires
also that the authority be effective in attaining that end. This demands that the organs through which the authority is institutional-
ized, becomes operative and pursues its ends, must be constituted
and act in such a manner as to be capable of bringing to realization
the new meaning which the common good is taking on in the historical evolution of the human family.

137. Today the universal common good poses problems of world-
wide dimensions which cannot be adequately tackled or solved
except by the efforts of public authorities endowed with a breadth
of powers, structure and means of the same proportions: that is, of
public authorities which are in a position to act in an effective
manner on a world-wide basis. The moral order itself, therefore,
demands that such a form of public authority be established.

PUBLIC AUTHORITY INSTITUTED BY
COMMON CONSENT, NOT IMPOSED BY FORCE

138. A public authority, having world-wide power and endowed
with the proper means for the efficacious pursuit of its objective,
which is the universal common good in concrete form, must be set
up by common accord and not imposed by force.

The reason is that such an authority must be in a position to
operate effectively, while at the same time its action must be inspired by sincere and real impartiality. In other words, it must be

an action aimed at satisfying the objective requirements of the universal common good.

The difficulty is that there would be reason to fear that a supranational or world-wide public authority, forcibly imposed by the more powerful political communities, might become an instrument of one-sided interests. And even should this not happen, it would be difficult for it to avoid all suspicion of partiality in its actions, and this would take away from its effectiveness.

Even though there may be pronounced differences between political communities as regards the degree of their economic development and their military power, they are all very sensitive as regards their juridical equality and their moral dignity. For that reason, they are right in not easily yielding in obedience to an authority imposed by force, or to an authority in whose creation they had no part or to which they themselves did not decide to submit by conscious and free choice.

THE UNIVERSAL COMMON GOOD AND PERSONAL RIGHTS

139. Like the common good of individual political communities, so too the universal common good cannot be determined except by having regard to the human person. Therefore, the public authority of the world community, too, must have as its fundamental objective the recognition, respect, safeguarding and promotion of the rights of the human person. This can be done by direct action when required, or by creating on a world scale an environment in which the public authorities of the individual political communities can more easily carry out their specific functions.

PRINCIPLE OF SUBSIDIARITY

140. Just as within each political community the relations between individuals, families, intermediate associations and public authority are governed by the principle of subsidiarity, so too the relations between the public authority of each political community and the public authority of the world community must be regulated by the same principle. This means that the public authority of the world community must tackle and solve problems of an economic, social,

political or cultural character which are posed by the universal common good. For, because of the vastness, complexity and urgency of those problems, the public authorities of the individual states are not in a position to tackle them with any hope of a positive solution.

141. The public authority of the world community is not intended to limit the sphere of action of the public authority of the individual political community, much less to take its place. On the contrary, its purpose is to create, on a world basis, an environment in which the public authorities of each political community, its citizens and intermediate associations, can carry out their tasks, fulfill their duties and exercise their rights with greater security.[64]

Signs of the Times

142. As is known, the United Nations (UN) was established on June 26, 1945, and to it there were subsequently added intergovernmental agencies with extensive international tasks in the economic, social, cultural, educational and health fields. The United Nations had as its essential purpose the maintenance and consolidation of peace between peoples, fostering between them friendly relations based on the principles of equality, mutual respect and varied forms of co-operation in every sector of human endeavor.

143. An act of the highest importance performed by the United Nations was the Universal Declaration of Human Rights, approved in the General Assembly on December 10, 1948. In the preamble of that declaration, the recognition and respect of those rights and respective liberties is proclaimed as an ideal to be pursued by all peoples and all countries.

144. Some objections and reservations, We observed, were raised regarding certain points in the declaration, and rightly so. There is no doubt, however, that the document represents an important step on the path toward the juridico-political organization of the world community. For in it, in most solemn form, the dignity of a human person is acknowledged in all men. And as a consequence there is proclaimed, as a fundamental right, the right of free movement in the search for truth and in the attainment of moral good and of justice, and also the right to a dignified life, while other rights connected with those mentioned are likewise proclaimed.

145. It is Our earnest prayer that the United Nations—in its structure and in its means—may become ever more equal to the magnitude and mobility of its tasks. May the day come as quickly as possible when every human being will find therein an effective safeguard for the rights which derive directly from his dignity as a person, and which are therefore universal, inviolable and inalienable rights. This is all the more to be hoped for since all human beings, as they take an ever more active part in the public life of their own political communities, are showing an increasing interest in the affairs of all peoples, and are becoming more consciously aware that they are living members of a world community.

Reprinted from Walter M. Abbott, S. J., ed., *The Documents of Vatican II* (New York: The America Press, 1966).

C.

Statement of Vatican II on War. From the Pastoral Constitution on the Church in the Modern World, Sections 79 through 82.

Curbing the Savagery of War

In spite of the fact that recent wars have wrought physical and moral havoc on our world, conflicts still produce their devastating effect day by day somewhere in the world. Indeed, now that every kind of weapon produced by modern science is used in war, the fierce character of warfare threatens to lead the combatants to a savagery far surpassing that of the past. Furthermore, the complexity of the modern world and the intricacy of international relations allow guerrilla warfare to be drawn out by new methods of deceit and subversion. In many cases the use of terrorism is regarded as a new way to wage war.

Contemplating this melancholy state of humanity, the Council wishes to recall first of all the permanent binding force of universal natural law and its all-embracing principles. Man's conscience itself gives ever more emphatic voice to these principles. Therefore, ac-

tions which deliberately conflict with these same principles, as well as orders commanding such actions, are criminal. Blind obedience cannot excuse those who yield to them. Among such must first be counted those actions designed for the methodical extermination of an entire people, nation, or ethnic minority. These actions must be vehemently condemned as horrendous crimes. The courage of those who openly and fearlessly resist men who issue such commands merits supreme commendation.

On the subject of war, quite a large number of nations have subscribed to various international agreements aimed at making military activity and its consequences less inhuman. Such are conventions concerning the handling of wounded or captured soldiers, and various similar agreements. Agreements of this sort must be honored. Indeed they should be improved upon so that they can better and more workably lead to restraining the frightfulness of war.

All men, especially government officials and experts in these matters, are bound to do everything they can to effect these improvements. Moreover, it seems right that laws make humane provisions for the case of those who for reasons of conscience refuse to bear arms, provided however, that they accept some other form of service to the human community.

Certainly, war has not been rooted out of human affairs. As long as the danger of war remains and there is no competent and sufficiently powerful authority at the international level, governments cannot be denied the right to legitimate defense once every means of peaceful settlement has been exhausted. Therefore, government authorities and others who share public responsibility have the duty to protect the welfare of the people entrusted to their care and to conduct such grave matters soberly.

But it is one thing to undertake military action for the just defense of the people, and something else again to seek the subjugation of other nations. Nor does the possession of war potential make every military or political use of it lawful. Neither does the mere fact that war has unhappily begun mean that all is fair between the warring parties.

Those who are pledged to the service of their country as members of its armed forces should regard themselves as agents of security and freedom on behalf of their people. As long as they fulfill this role properly, they are making a genuine contribution to the establishment of peace.

Total War

The horror and perversity of war are immensely magnified by the multiplication of scientific weapons. For acts of war involving these weapons can inflict massive and indiscriminate destruction far exceeding the bounds of legitimate defense. Indeed, if the kind of instruments which can now be found in the armories of the great nations were to be employed to their fullest, an almost total and altogether reciprocal slaughter of each side by the other would follow, not to mention the widespread devastation which would take place in the world and the deadly aftereffects which would be spawned by the use of such weapons.

All these considerations compel us to undertake an evaluation of war with an entirely new attitude. The men of our time must realize that they will have to give a somber reckoning for their deeds of war. For the course of the future will depend largely on the decisions they make today.

With these truths in mind, this most holy Synod makes its own the condemnations of total war already pronounced by recent Popes and issues the following declaration:

Any act of war aimed indiscriminately at the destruction of entire cities or of extensive areas along with their population is a crime against God and man himself. It merits unequivocal and unhesitating condemnation.

The unique hazard of modern warfare consists in this: it provides those who possess modern scientific weapons with a kind of occasion for perpetrating just such abominations. Moreover, through a certain inexorable chain of events, it can urge men on to the most atrocious decisions. That such in fact may never happen in the future, the bishops of the whole world, in unity assembled, beg all men, especially government officials and military leaders, to give unremitting thought to the awesome responsibility which is theirs before God and the entire human race.

The Arms Race

Scientific weapons, to be sure, are not amassed solely for use in war. The defensive strength of any nation is considered to be dependent upon its capacity for immediate retaliation against an adversary. Hence this accumulation of arms, which increases each year, also serves, in a way heretofore unknown, as a deterrent to possible enemy attack. Many regard this state of affairs as the most effective way by which peace of a sort can be maintained between nations at the present time.

Whatever be the case with this method of deterrence, men should be convinced that the arms race in which so many countries are engaged is not a safe way to preserve a steady peace. Nor is the so-called balance resulting from this race a sure and authentic peace. Rather than being eliminated thereby, the causes of war threaten to grow gradually stronger.

While extravagant sums are being spent for the furnishing of ever new weapons, an adequate remedy cannot be provided for the multiple miseries afflicting the whole modern world. Disagreements between nations are not really and radically healed. On the contrary other parts of the world are infected with them. New approaches initiated by reformed attitudes must be adopted to remove this trap and to restore genuine peace by emancipating the world from its crushing anxiety.

Therefore, it must be said again: the arms race is an utterly treacherous trap for humanity, and one which injures the poor to an intolerable degree. It is much to be feared that if this race persists, it will eventually spawn all the lethal ruin whose path it is now making ready.

Warned by the calamities which the human race has made possible, let us make use of the interlude granted us from above and in which we rejoice. In greater awareness of our own responsibility let us find means for resolving our disputes in a manner more worthy of man. Divine Providence urgently demands of us that we free ourselves from the age-old slavery of war. But if we refuse to make this effort, we do not know where the evil road we have ventured upon will lead us.

The Total Banning of War, and
the International Action for Avoiding War

It is our clear duty, then, to strain every muscle as we work for the time when all war can be completely outlawed by international consent. This goal undoubtedly requires the establishment of some universal public authority acknowledged as such by all, and endowed with effective power to safeguard, on the behalf of all, security, regard for justice, and respect for rights.

But before this hoped-for authority can be set up, the highest existing international centers must devote themselves vigorously to the pursuit of better means for obtaining common security. Peace must be born of mutual trust between nations rather than imposed on them through fear of one another's weapons. Hence everyone must labor to put an end at last to the arms race, and to make a true beginning of disarmament, not indeed a unilateral disarmament, but one proceeding at an equal pace according to agreement, and backed up by authentic and workable safeguards.

In the meantime, efforts which have already been made and are still under way to eliminate the danger of war are not to be underrated. On the contrary, support should be given to the good will of the very many leaders who work hard to do away with war, which they abominate. Though burdened by the enormous preoccupations of their high office, these men are nonetheless motivated by the very grave peacemaking task to which they are bound, even if they cannot ignore the complexity of matters as they stand.

We should fervently ask God to give these men the strength to go forward perseveringly and to follow through courageously on this work of building peace with vigor. It is a work of supreme love for mankind. Today it most certainly demands that these leaders extend their thoughts and their spirit beyond the confines of their own nation, that they put aside national selfishness and ambition to dominate other nations, and that they nourish a profound reverence for the whole of humanity, which is already making its way so laboriously toward greater unity.

The problems of peace and of disarmament have already been the subject of extensive, strenuous, and relentless examination. Together with international meetings dealing with these problems, such studies should be regarded as the first steps toward solving these serious questions. They should be promoted with even greater urgency in the hope that they will yield practical results in the future.

Nevertheless, men should take heed not to entrust themselves only to the efforts of others, while remaining careless about their own attitudes. For government officials, who must simultaneously guarantee the good of their own people and promote the universal good, depend on public opinion and feeling to the greatest possible extent. It does them no good to work at building peace so long as feelings of hostility, contempt, and distrust, as well as racial hatred and unbending ideologies, continue to divide men and place them in opposing camps.

Hence arises a surpassing need for renewed education of attitudes and for new inspiration in the area of public opinion. Those who are dedicated to the work of education, particularly of the young, or who mold public opinion, should regard as their most weighty task the effort to instruct all in fresh sentiments of peace. Indeed, every one of us should have a change of heart as we regard the entire world and those tasks which we can perform in unison for the betterment of our race.

But we should not let false hope deceive us. For enmities and hatred must be put away and firm, honest agreements concerning world peace reached in the future. Otherwise, for all its marvelous knowledge, humanity, which is already in the middle of a grave crisis, will perhaps be brought to that mournful hour in which it will experience no peace other than the dreadful peace of death.

But, while we say this, the Church of Christ takes her stand in the midst of the anxiety of this age, and does not cease to hope with the utmost confidence. She intends to propose to our age over and over again, in season and out of season, this apostolic message: "Behold, now is the acceptable time" for a change of heart; "behold now is the day of salvation!"

Reprinted from Walter M. Abbott, S.J., ed., *The Documents of Vatican II* (New York: The America Press, 1966).

D.

Statement of the American Bishops on Peace November, 1966

OUR COMMON HUMANITY demands that all people live in peace and harmony with one another. This peace will exist only if the right order established by God is observed, an order which is based on the requirements of human dignity. Everyone, therefore, must be vitally and personally concerned about correcting the grave disorders which today threaten peace. As Catholics we are members of the Church which Pope Paul has called a "messenger of peace."

We, the Catholic Bishops of the United States, consider it our duty to help magnify the moral voice of our nation. This voice, fortunately, is becoming louder and clearer because it is the voice of all faiths. To the strong words of the National Council of Churches, the Synagogue Council of America and other religious bodies, we add our own pleas for peace. Our approaches may at times differ, but our starting point (justice) and our goal (peace) do not.

While we cannot resolve all the issues involved in the Vietnam

190

conflict, it is clearly our duty to insist that they be kept under constant moral scrutiny. No one is free to evade his personal responsibility by leaving it entirely to others to make moral judgments. In this connection, the Vatican Council warns that "men should heed not to entrust themselves only to the efforts of others, while remaining careless about their own attitudes. For government officials, who must simultaneously guarantee the good of their own people and promote the universal good, depend on public opinion and feeling to the greatest possible extent." (*Constitution on the Church in the Modern World,* §82)

While it is not possible in this brief statement to give a detailed analysis of the Church's total teaching on war and peace, it seems necessary to review certain basic principles if the present crisis is to be put in its proper moral perspectives.

We reaffirmed at the Council the legitimate role of patriotism for the well-being of a nation, but a clear distinction was made between true and false patriotism: "Citizens should develop a generous and loyal devotion to their country, but without any narrowing of mind. In other words, they must always look simultaneously to the welfare of the whole human family, which is tied together by the manifold bonds linking races, peoples and nations." (*Ibid.,* §75).

But these limits on patriotism do not rule out a country's right to legitimate self-defense. While making it clear that all means short of force must first be used, the Council restated the traditional teaching regarding the right of self-defense: "As long as the danger of war remains and there is no competent and sufficiently powerful authority at the international level, government cannot be denied the right to legitimate defense." (*Ibid.,* §79) And what a nation can do to defend itself it may do to help another in its struggle against aggression.

In the conduct of any war, there may be moral limits: "Any act of war aimed indiscriminately at the destruction of entire cities or of extensive areas along with their population is a crime against God and man himself. It merits unequivocal and unhesitating condemnation." (*Ibid.,* §80). Moreover, as the Council also reminded us, the fact that a war of self-defense has unhappily begun does not mean that any and all means may be employed by the warring parties.

While the stockpiling of scientific weapons serves, for the present, as a deterrent to aggression, the Council has warned us that "the arms race in which so many countries are engaged is not a safe way to preserve a steady peace." (*Ibid.*, §81) Indeed, it is a "treacherous trap for humanity." Far from promoting a sure and authentic peace, it actually fosters war by diverting resources which could be better used to alleviate the human misery which causes war. In their urgent plea for disarmament, however, the Council fathers understood that it will be effective only if it is universal and if there are adequate means of enforcing it.

The Council commended those citizens who defend their nation against aggression. They are "instruments of security and freedom on behalf of their people. As long as they fulfill the role properly, they are making a genuine contribution to the establishment of peace." (*Ibid.*, §79) At the same time, however, it pointed out that some provision should be made for those who conscientiously object to bearing arms: "It seems right that laws make humane provisions for the care of those who for reasons of conscience refuse to bear arms; provided, however, that they accept some other form of service to the human community." (*Ibid.*, §79).

In light of these principles, how are we as Americans to judge the involvement of the United States in Vietnam? What can we do to promote peace?

Americans can have confidence in the sincerity of their leaders as long as they work for a just peace in Vietnam. Their efforts to find a solution to the present impasse are well known. We realize that citizens of all faiths and of differing political loyalties honestly differ among themselves over the moral issues involved in this tragic conflict. While we do not claim to be able to resolve these issues authoritatively, in the light of the facts as they are known to us, it is reasonable to argue that our presence in Vietnam is justified. We share the anguish of our government officials in their awesome responsibility of making life-and-death decisions about our national policy in Vietnam. We commend the valor of our men in the armed forces, and we express to them our debt of gratitude. In our time, thousands of men have given their lives in war. To those who loved them, we express our sorrow at their loss and promise our constant prayer.

But we cannot stop here. While we can conscientiously support the position of our country in the present circumstances, it is the duty of everyone to search for other alternatives. And everyone— government leaders and citizens alike—must be prepared to change our course whenever a change in circumstances warrants it.

This can be done effectively only if we know the facts and issue involved. Within the limits imposed by our national security, there- fore, we must always insist that these facts and issues be made known to the public so that they can be considered in their moral context.

On the basis of our knowledge and understanding of the current situation, we are also bound always to make sure that our govern- ment does, in fact, pursue every possibility which offers even the slightest hope of a peaceful settlement. And we must clearly protest whenever there is a danger that the conflict will be escalated beyond morally acceptable limits.

On a broader level, we must support our government in its efforts to negotiate a workable formula for disarmament. What we seek is not unilateral disarmament, but one proceeding, in the words of the Council, "at an equal pace according to agreement, and backed up by authentic and workable safeguards." (*Ibid.*, §82) We commend the officials of our country and others for their contribution to the proposed Treaty Against Nuclear Proliferation which, hopefully, will soon become a reality.

Moreover, we must use every resource available, as a nation, to help alleviate the basic cause of war. If the God-given dignity of the people of poorer nations is not to become an illusion, these nations must be able to provide for the spiritual and material needs of their citizens. We must help them do this. The economically developed nations of the world, as Pope John insisted in his great encyclical, *Pacem in Terris,* must come to the aid of those which are in the process of developing so that every man, woman and child in the world may be able "to live in conditions more in keeping with their human dignity."(*Pacem in Terris*)

There is a grave danger that the circumstances of the present war in Vietnam may, in time, diminish our moral sensitivity to its evils. Every means at our disposal, therefore, must be used to create a climate of peace. In this climate, prayer, personal example, study, discussion and lectures can strengthen the will for peace. We must advocate what we believe are the best methods of promoting peace: mutual agreements, safeguards and inspection; the creation of an international public authority to negotiate toward peace. Above all, in its peace-making efforts, we must support the work of the United Nations which, in the words of Pope Paul, marks "a stage in the development of mankind, from which retreat must never be admitted, but from which it is necessary that advance be made." (address to the General Assembly of the United Nations Oct. 4, 1965).

We ask every person of good will to support with prayer the Holy Father's plea for a Christmas cease-fire. May it open the way to lasting peace. In the spirit of Christ, the Christian must be the persistent seeker in the Gospel, the man willing to walk the second mile. (cf. Matt 5:42) He walks prudently, but he walks generously and he asks that all men do the same.

As Catholics we walk in good company. Pope Paul, in his recent encyclical on peace, cried out, in God's name, to stop war. We pray that the sacrifices of us all, our prayers as well as our faltering efforts toward peace, will hasten the day when the whole world will echo Pope Paul's historic words: "No more war, war never again!" (*Ibid.*)

Reprinted from the *Catholic Mind* (February, 1967).

E.

Statement of the American Bishops on

Peace and War

November, 1968

The Family of Nations

We share the deep concern of thoughtful people in our times, a concern voiced by the Vatican Council, that "the whole human family has reached an hour of supreme crisis" (*Gaudium et Spes*, §77). The crisis can ultimately offer great promise for a more abundant human life, but at the moment it portends grave threats to all life. The threats to life depend on urgent and difficult decisions concerning war and peace. In considering these we share the conviction of Vatican Council II that the horror and perversity of technological warfare "compel us to undertake an evaluation of war *with an entirely new attitude*" (§80, emphasis added).

This compelling obligation is the greater in our case since we are citizens of a nation in many ways the most powerful in the world. The responsibility of moral leadership is the greater in the local Church of a nation whose arsenals contain the greatest nuclear potential for both the harm that we would wish to impede or the help it is our obligation to encourage. We are acutely aware that our moral posture and comportment in this hour of supreme crisis will be assessed by the judgment of history and of God.

We renew the affirmation by the Council that "the loftier strivings and aspirations of the human race are in harmony with the message of the Gospel" (§77). We speak as witnesses to the Gospel, aware that the issues of war and peace test the relevancy of its message for our generation, particularly in terms of the service of life and its dignity. We seek to speak in the spirit of that Gospel message, which is at heart a doctrine of nonviolence rather than violence, of peace understood as Jesus proclaimed it (cf, John 14:27).

We call upon American Catholics to evaluate war with that "entirely new attitude" for which the Council appealed and which may rightly be expected of all who, calling themselves Christians, proclaim their identity with the Prince of Peace. We share with all men of good will the conviction that a more humane society will not come "unless each person devotes himself with renewed determination to the cause of peace" (§77). We appeal to policy makers and statesmen to reflect soberly on the Council teaching concerning peace and war, and vigorously to pursue the search for means by which at all times to limit and eventually to outlaw the destructiveness of war.

The Vatican Council noted that "war continues to produce daily devastation in one or another part of the world" (§79). The observation has lost none of its truth in the period since the Council ended; indeed, there have been further grievous outbreaks of war and aggression.

Of one mind with the Council, we condemn without qualification wars of aggression however their true character may sometimes be veiled. Whatever case there may have seemed to exist in other times for wars fought for the domination of another nation, such a case can no longer be imagined given the circumstances of modern warfare, the heightened sense of international mutuality and the increasingly available humane means to the realization of that mutuality.

We join wholeheartedly in the Council's condemnation of wars fought without limitation. We recognize the right of legitimate self-defense, and, in a world society still unorganized, the necessity for recourse to armed defense and to collective security action in the absence of a competent authority on the international level and once peaceful means have been exhausted. But we seek to limit warfare and to humanize it, where it remains a last resort, in the maximum degree possible. Most of all, we urge the enlisting of the energies of all men of good will in forging the instruments of peace, to the end that war may at long last be outlawed.

Meanwhile, we are gratefully conscious that "those who are pledged to the service of their country as members of its armed forces should regard themselves as agents of security and freedom on behalf of their people. As long as they fulfill their role properly, they are making a genuine contribution to the establishment of peace" (*Gaudium et Spes*, §79).

In the Christian message peace is not merely the absence of war. Ultimately, of course, it presupposes that presence within and among men of a positive principle of life and unity, which is none other than the divine life to which the Church bears witness, of which Christ in His Church is the source. The soul, then, of a peaceful society is divine charity. But justice, the great concern of the well-ordered state and the justification for its existence, is the foundation of organized society.

Therefore, peace cannot be reduced solely to the maintenance of a balance of power between enemies; nor is it to be brought about by dictatorship, whether this be the imposition of the sheer will of a ruler, a party or even a majority. It is an enterprise of justice and must be built up ceaselessly in seeking to satisfy the all-embracing demands of the common good. This is the point of Pope Paul's positive, dynamic concept of peace: the modern word for peace is development. Peace therefore presupposes the fraternal confidence which manifests itself in a firm determination to respect other persons and peoples, above all their human dignity, and to collaborate with them in the pursuit of the shared hopes of mankind.

ARMS CONTROL

It is in nuclear warfare, even in its "cold" phase or form, that mankind confronts the moral issue of modern war in its extreme case. This has become a situation in which two adversaries possess and deploy weapons which, if used against each other, could annihilate their respective civilizations and even threaten the survival of the human race. Nothing more dramatically suggests the antilife direction of technological warfare than the neutron bomb; one philosopher declares that the manner in which it would leave entire cities intact, but totally without life, makes it, perhaps, the symbol of our civilization. It would be perverse indeed if the Christian conscience were to be unconcerned or mute in the face of the multiple moral aspects of these awesome prospects.

It is now a quarter century since Pope Pius XII summoned that conscience to a "war on war." He pointed out World War II's "unspeakable atrocities," the "image of a hell upon which anyone who nourishes humane sentiments in his heart can have no more ardent wish than to close the door forever." He warned against the further progress of "human inventions ... directed to destruction," and pleaded that to the recognition of the immorality of wars of aggression there be added "the threat of a judicial intervention of the nations and of a punishment inflicted on the aggressor by the United Nations, so that war may always feel itself proscribed, always under the watchful guard of preventive action." He argued that then "humanity, issuing from the dark night in which it has been submerged for so great a length of time, will be able to greet the dawn of a new and better era in its history" (Christmas Broadcast, 1944).

The Second Vatican Council, in a solemn declaration, endorsed "the condemnation of total warfare issued by recent popes" and stated: "Every act of war directed to the indiscriminate destruction of whole cities or vast areas with their inhabitants is a crime against God and man which merits firm and unequivocal condemnation" (*Gaudium et Spes*, §80).

The Council explicitly condemned the use of weapons of mass destruction, but abstained from condemning the *possession* of such weapons to deter "possible enemy attack" (§81). Though not passing direct judgment on this strategy of deterrence, the Council did declare that "men should be convinced that the arms race in which so many countries are engaged is not a safe way to preserve a steady peace. Nor is the so-called "balance" resulting from the race a pure and authentic peace. Rather than being eliminated thereby, the causes of war threaten to grow gradually stronger ... Therefore it must be said again: the arms race is an utterly treacherous trap for humanity, and one which ensnares the poor to an intolerable degree" (§81).

The Council did not call for unilateral disarmament; Christian morality is not lacking in realism. But it did call for reciprocal or collective disarmament "proceeding at an equal pace according to agreement and backed up by authentic and workable safeguards" (§82). There are hopeful signs that such a formula may be strengthened by the Partial Test Ban Treaty and that the commitment under the Non-Proliferation Treaty to proceed to a negotiation of balanced reductions of nuclear weapons—at the same time extending the use of nuclear power for peaceful development of the needy nations under adequate inspection safeguards—may provide a positive, sane pattern for the future. We earnestly pray so, commending the furtherance of these hopes to responsible political leaders and to the support of all citizens.

Meanwhile, it is greatly to be desired that such prospects not be dashed by irrational resolves to keep ahead in "assured destruction" capability. Rather it is to be hoped that the early ratification by the Senate of the Non-Proliferation Treaty—which in essence is a Treaty between the U.S.S.R. and the U.S. and other nations—will hasten discussion of across the board reductions by the big powers. Despite, and even because of the provocations in Eastern Europe and elsewhere, the United States should continue steps to create a better climate for these discussions, such as taking the lead in inviting the UN Atomic Energy Commission and other organizations and foreign states to visit its nuclear facilities, and scrupulously reviewing all commitments for the sale, loan or lease of armaments.

The Council's position on the arms race was clear. To recall it: "Therefore, we declare once again: the arms race is an utterly treacherous trap for humanity ... It is much to be feared that if this race persists, it will eventually spawn all the lethal ruin whose path it is now making ready" (§81).

Nonetheless, the nuclear race goes on. The latest act in the continuing nuclear arms race is no doubt the U.S. decision to build a "thin" antiballistic missile system to defend against possible nuclear attack by another world power. This decision has been widely interpreted as the prelude to a "thick" ABM system to defend against possible nuclear attack.

In themselves, such antiballistic missiles are purely defensive, designed to limit the damage to the United States from nuclear attack. Nevertheless, by upsetting the present strategic balance, the so-called balance of terror, there is grave danger that a United States ABM system will incite other nations to increase their offensive nuclear forces with the seeming excuse of a need to restore the balance.

Despite the danger of triggering an expanded escalation of the arms race the pressures for a "thick" ABM deployment persist.

We seriously question whether the present policy of maintaining nuclear superiority is meaningful for security. There is no advantage to be gained by nuclear superiority, however it is computed, when each side is admittedly capable of inflicting overwhelming damage on the other, even after being attacked first. Such effective parity has been operative for some years. Any effort to achieve superiority only leads to ever-higher levels of armaments as it forces the side with the lesser capability to seek to maintain its superiority. In the wake of this action-reaction phenomenon comes a decrease in both stability and security.

The National Conference of Catholic Bishops pledges its united effort toward forming a climate of public opinion for peace, mindful of the Council's advice that "government officials ... depend on public opinion and feeling to the greatest possible extent" (§82). We will therefore, through existing and improved agencies, support national programs of education for Catholic Americans and for all Americans in collaboration with all religious groups as well as with other organizations.

With *Gaudium et Spes,* we commend the arduous and unceasing efforts of statesmen and specialists in the field of arms control and disarmament, and add our own encouragement of systematic studies in this field. As the Council appealed to Catholic scholars throughout the world to participate more fully in such studies, so we call upon intellectuals in the Church in our land to bring scholarly competence and their powers of persuasion to that "war on war" which the modern Popes have without exception pleaded that we wage.

We urge Catholics, and indeed all our countrymen, to make a ceaseless vigil of prayers for peace and for all those who are charged with the delicate and difficult negotiations of disarmament. Such prayers provide the most obvious and appropriate occasion for ecumenical services bringing together all in our communities who cherish the blessed vision of peace heralded by the Hebrew prophets and preached by Christ and His Apostles. We cannot but question the depth of the commitment to peace of people of religious background who no longer pray for peace. But those who only pray for peace, leaving to others the arduous work for peace, the dialogue for peace, have a defective theology concerning the relation between human action and the accomplishment of that will of God in which is our peace. So, too, those who, neglectful of the part of prayer, rely only on their own power, or on the pooling of merely human resources or intelligence, energy and even good will, forget the wisdom of Scripture: "If the Lord does not build the house, in vain the masons toil; if the Lord does not guard the city, in vain the sentries watch" (Psalm 127, 1-2).

THE INTERNATIONAL COMMUNITY

The Council Fathers recognized that not even ending the nuclear arms race, which itself cannot be accomplished without the full co-operation of the international community, would ensure the permanent removal of the awesome threat of modern war. Nor would disarmament alone, even assuming it to be complete and across the board, remove the causes of war. "This goal undoubtedly requires the establishment of some universal public authority acknowledged as such by all, and endowed with effective power to safeguard, on the behalf of all, security, regard for justice and respect for rights" (§82).

Such an authority, furthermore, is required by the growing, ever more explicit interdependence of all men and nations as a result of which the common good "today takes on an increasingly universal complexion and consequently involves rights and duties with respect to the whole human race" (§26).

Therefore political leaders should "extend their thoughts and their spirit beyond the confines of their own nation, put aside national selfishness and ambition to dominate other nations, and nourish a profound reverence for the whole of humanity, always making its way so laboriously toward greater unity" (§82).

We commend the efforts of world statesmen, particularly those of our own nation, who seek to extend the spirit and practice of cooperation in international agencies and regional associations of nations, with the object not only of terminating or preventing war, and of building up a body of international law, but also of removing the causes of war through positive programs.

Since war remains a melancholy fact of life today, we believe the United States not only should insist on adherence to and the application by all nations of existing international conventions or treaties on the laws of war, such as the revised Geneva Convention relative to the treatment of prisoners of war, but should take the lead in seeking to update them. Certain forms of warfare, new and old, should be outlawed, and practices in dealing with civilian populations, prisoners of war and refugees are always in need of review and reform.

Here, too, our dependence on responsible writers, informed speakers and competent critics is crucial to the cause of peace. Hence, we encourage Catholic scholars to undertake systematic studies of new developments, theories and practices in warfare, including guerrilla warfare, revolution and "wars of liberation." Changing political patterns, improved techniques of communication, new methods of remote controls and of surveillance of individuals and communities alike made possible by science, as well as shifting ethical standards, make it the vocation of devout intellectuals, both as citizens of their own nations and servants of the common good of mankind, to bring informed competence to the illumination, discussion and resolution of the complex issues, many of them moral, arising from all these.

A Catholic position of opposition to compulsory peacetime military service, first formulated on the level of the Holy See by Pope Benedict XV, has had for its premise the fact that such service has been a contributing cause of the breeding of actual wars, a part of the "great armaments" and "armed peace" security concept, and, in the words of Cardinal Gasparri in a letter to Lloyd George, the cause of such great evils for more than a century that the cure of these evils can only be found in the suppression of this system. In the spirit of this position, we welcome the voices lifted up among our political leaders which ask for a total review of the draft system and the establishment of voluntary military service in a professional army with democratic safeguards and for clear purposes of adequate defense. Our call for the end of any draft system at home which, in practice, amounts at times to compulsory peacetime military service is in direct line with previous resolutions of the hierarchy of the United States on compulsory military training.

Apart from the question of war itself, we deem it opportune here to reiterate the Council's condemnation of genocide, the methodical extermination of an entire people, nation or ethnic minority for reasons connected with race, religion or status such as that undertaken by the Nazis against the Jews among their own citizens and later against all the Jewish people, as well as so-called "gypsies." We would urge United States ratification of the United Nations Convention on this subject and of every other sound implementing instrument by which the United Nations Declaration of Human Rights can be translated from the level of ideals to that of actuality. Furthermore, we urge increased support by our own countrymen and citizens of all nations of all international programs consistent with the protection and promotion of the sanctity of human life and the dignity of the human persons in times of war and peace.

We earnestly appeal to our own government and to all governments to give the elimination of the present international "war system" a priority consistent with the damaging effect of massive armament programs on all the objectives of the good society to which enlightened governments give priorities: education, public health, a true sense of security, prosperity, maximum liberty, the flourishing of the humane arts and sciences, in a word the service of life itself. Thus can we strive to move away, as reason and religion demand, from the "war system" to an international system in which unilateral recourse to force is increasingly restricted.

This will require international peacemaking and peace-keeping machinery. To this end we urge all to support efforts for a stronger and more effective United Nations that it may become a true instrument of peace and justice among nations. In this respect the peace motivation of Pope Paul's public support of the United Nations by his moral authority and teaching office at the time of his visit to that body on its anniversary should be normative for Catholics.

We would welcome in official pronouncements of our own and other governments, as well as in the increased support given to the United Nations and associated agencies by the citizens of all nations, a greater interest in and direction toward the establishment of that universal public authority which the Council Fathers urged.

We recognize that any use of police action by such an international authority, or, in the meantime, by the UN as presently constituted, or by duly constituted regional agencies, must be carefully subject to covenants openly arrived at and freely accepted, covenants spelling out clear norms such as that of proportionate force; here, again, the work of qualified and conscientious specialists is indispensable.

Turning to the more positive aspects of the building of an international community and the duties of us as Americans in this matter, we deplore the lack of a stable, persevering national concern for the promotion of the international common good. This is reflected in the fickleness of public interest in and Congressional support of foreign aid. It is reflected also in a seeming insensitivity to the importance of trade agreements beneficial to developing nations. A like lack of generosity, dangerous to the fully human common good, is present in the increasingly bold linking of contraceptive programs, even when superficially voluntary, to needed aid programs. Future aid and trade assistance programs should become increasingly multilateral; they should never merely serve national self-interest except to the extent that national interest is genuinely part and parcel of the general good of the human community.

Because of the war in Vietnam, and the growing preoccupation with the social problems of our cities, there is the peril of an upsurge of exaggerated forms of nationalism and isolationism which the teachings of all churches reprove and the experiences of World War II had, we hoped, forever discredited.

It is the duty of our political leadership, of citizens, and especially of believers who acknowledge the brotherhood of man, to promote and develop the spirit of international concern, co-operation and understanding.

As the Council noted: "There arises a surpassing need for renewed education of attitudes and for new inspiration in the area of public opinion. Those who are dedicated to the work of education, particularly of the young, or who mold public opinion should regard as their most weighty task the effort to instruct all in fresh sentiments of peace" (§82).

To assist the agencies and institutions of the Catholic Church in the United States in their response to this "most weighty task," the Catholic Bishops have recently established a Division of World Justice and Peace, corresponding to the newly established Vatican Commission. It is our desire that the Division will stimulate renewed efforts in this field, and co-ordinate whenever possible such efforts with those of other Christian bodies in an ecumenical framework. We call upon all men of conscience, all public spirited citizens, to dedicate themselves with fresh energy to this work.

We believe that the talents and resources of our land are so abundant that we may promote the common good of nations at no expense to the vitally necessary works of urban and rural reconstruction in our own country. The latter are the first order of domestic policy, just as the former should be the first order of foreign policy. Neither should be neglected, both being equally urgent; in the contemporary and developing world order their fortunates are intertwined.

VIETNAM

In a previous statement we ventured a tentative judgment that, on balance, the U.S. presence in Vietnam was useful and justified.

Since then American Catholics have entered vigorously into the national debate on this question, which, explicitly or implicitly, is going deeply into the moral aspect of our involvement in Vietnam. In this debate, opinions among Catholics appear as varied as in our society as a whole; one cannot accuse Catholics of either being partisans of any one point of view or of being unconcerned. In our democratic system the fundamental right of political dissent cannot be denied, nor is rational debate on public policy decisions of government in the light of moral and political principles to be discouraged. It is the duty of the governed to analyze responsibily the concrete issue of public policy.

In assessing our country's involvement in Vietnam we must ask:

Have we already reached, or passed, the point where the principle of proportionality becomes decisive? How much more of our resources in men and money should we commit to this struggle, assuming an acceptable cause or intention? Has the conflict in Vietnam provoked inhuman dimensions of suffering? Would not an untimely withdrawal be equally disastrous?

Granted that financial considerations are necessarily subordinate to ethical values in any moral question, nonetheless many wonder if perhaps a measure of the proportions in this, as in any modern war, may be reflected in the amounts inevitably lost to education, poverty-relief and positive works of social justice at home and abroad (including Southeast Asia) as a result of the mounting budgets for this and like military operations. This point has frequently been raised by the Popes, notably by Pope Pius XII who invoked the principle of proportionality in his analysis of the morality even of defensive wars, particularly when these involve ABC elements (atomic, biological, chemical) and losses disproportionate to the "injustice tolerated" (Address to Military Doctors, Oct. 19, 1953).

While it would be beyond our competence to propose any technical formulas for bringing the Vietnam War to an end, we welcome the bombing halt and pray for the success of the negotiations.

Meanwhile there are moral lessons to be learned from our involvement in Vietnam that will apply to future cases. One might be that military power and technology do not suffice, even with the strongest resolve, to restore order or accomplish peace. As a rule internal political conflicts are too complicated to be solved by the external application of force and technology.

Another might be the realization that some evils existing in the world, evils such as undernutrition, economic frustration, social stagnation and political injustices, may be more readily attacked and corrected through non-military means, than by military efforts to counteract the subversive forces bent on their exploitation.

In addition, may we not hope that violence will be universally discredited as a means of remedying human ills, and that the spirit of love "may overcome the barriers that divide, cherish the bonds of mutual charity, understand others and pardon those who have done them wrong"? (*Pacem in Terris,* §171).

THE ROLE OF CONSCIENCE

The war in Vietnam typifies the issues which present and future generations will be less willing to leave entirely to the normal political and bureaucratic processes of national decision-making. It is not surprising that those who are most critical, even intemperate in their discussion of war as an instrument of national policy, or as a ready means to the settling even of wrongs, are among the young; the burden of killing and dying falls principally on them.

There is sometimes ground for question as to whether the attitudes of some toward military duty do not spring from cowardice. In this problem, as in all crises which test generosity and heroism, cases of moral as well as physical cowardice doubtless occur. But a blanket charge of this kind would be unfair to those young people who are clearly willing to suffer social ostracism and even prison terms because of their opposition to a particular war. One must conclude that for many of our youthful protesters, the motives spring honestly from the principled opposition to a given war as pointless or immoral.

Nor can it be said that such conscientious objection to war, as war is waged in our times, is entirely the result of subjective considerations and without reference to the message of the Gospel and the teaching of the Church; quite the contrary, frequently conscientious dissent reflects the influence of the principles which inform modern papal teaching, the Pastoral Constitution and a classical tradition of moral doctrine in the Church, including, in fact, the norms for the moral evaluation of a theoretically just war.

The enthusiasm of many young people for new programs of service to fellow humans in need may be proof that some traditional forms of patriotism are in process of being supplemented by a new spirit of dedication to humanity and to the moral prestige of one's own nation. This new spirit must be taken seriously; it may not always match the heroism of the missionaries and the full measure of the life of faith, but it is not contradictory to these and may open up new forms of Christian apostolate.

As witnesses to a spiritual tradition which accepts enlightened conscience, even when honestly mistaken, as the immediate arbiter of moral decisions, we can only feel reassured by this evidence of individual responsibility and the decline of uncritical conformism to patterns, some of which included strong moral elements, to be sure, but also included political, social, cultural and like controls not necessarily in conformity with the mind and heart of the Church.

If war is ever to be outlawed, and replaced by more humane and enlightened institutions to regulate conflicts among nations, institutions rooted in the notion of universal common good, it will be because the citizens of this and other nations have rejected the tenets of exaggerated nationalism and insisted on principles of non-violent political and civic action in both the domestic and international spheres.

We therefore join with the Council Fathers in praising "those who renounce the use of violence in the vindication of their rights and who resort to methods of defense which are otherwise available to weaker parties, provided that this can be done without injury to the rights and duties of others or of the community itself " (§78).

It is this light that we seek to interpret and apply to our own situation the advice of the Vatican Council on the treatment of conscientious objectors. The Council endorses laws that "make humane provision for the care of those who for reasons of conscience refuse to bear arms, provided, however, that they accept some other form of service to the human community" (§79).

The present laws of this country, however, provide only for those whose reasons of conscience are grounded in a total rejection of the use of military force. This form of conscientious objection deserves the legal provision made for it, but we consider that the time has come to urge that similar consideration be given those whose reasons of conscience are more personal and specific.

We therefore recommend a modification of the Selective Service Act making it possible, although not easy, for so-called selective conscientious objectors to refuse—without fear of imprisonment or loss of citizenship—to serve in wars which they consider unjust or in branches of service (e.g., the strategic nuclear forces) which would subject them to the performance of actions contrary to deeply held moral convictions about indiscriminate killing. Some other form of service to the human community should be required of those so exempted.

Whether or not such modifications in our laws are in fact made, we continue to hope that, in the all-important issue of war and peace, all men will follow their consciences. We can do no better than to recall, as did the Vatican Council, "the permanent binding force of universal natural law and its all embracing principles," to which "man's conscience itself gives ever more emphatic voice."

In calling so persistently in this Pastoral for studies on the application of sound moral principles to new dimensions of changes in the problems of war and peace, we are mindful of our own responsibilty to proclaim the Gospel of peace and to teach the precepts of both natural and revealed divine law concerning the establishing of peace everywhere on earth (§79).

We therefore have made our own the Council's judgment on "the deeper causes of war," sins like envy, mistrust and egoism. We echo the warning given by Pope Paul at the United Nations: "Today as never before, in an era marked by such human progress, there is need for an appeal to the moral conscience of man. For the danger comes not from progress, nor from science—on the contrary, if properly utilized these could resolve many of the grave problems which beset mankind. The real danger comes from man himself, who has at his disposal ever more powerful instruments, which can be used as well for destruction as for the most lofty of conquests."

The hour has indeed struck for "conversion," for personal transformation, for interior renewal. We must once again begin to think of man in a new way, and of human life with a new appreciation of its worth, its dignity and its call to elevation to the level of the life of God Himself. All this requires that, with refreshed purpose and deepened faith, we follow the urging of St. Paul that we "put on the new man, which has been created according to God in justice and holiness of truth" (Eph. 4:23).

Conclusion

Christians believe God to be the "source of life" (cf. Jn. 5:26) and of love since "love comes from God" (cf. 1 Jn. 4:7). "God is love" (1 Jn. 4:8) and man has been made in His image and likeness (Genesis 1:26). Thus, man is most himself when he honors life and lives by love. Then he is most like to God.

The doctrine and defense of life require a renewed spirituality in the Church. Such a spirituality will reaffirm the sacred character of married love through which life is begun, the dignity of the family within which love brings life to maturity, and the blessed vision of peace in which life is shared by men and nations in a world community of love.

These themes, all of which touch on life, we have explored in terms of the family, the commonwealth of nations and some of the antilife forces which threaten these.

In her defense of human life the Church in our day makes her own, as did Moses, the words by which God Himself reduces our perplexities to a clear, inescapable choice: "I call heaven and earth to witness against you this day, that I have set before you life and death ... therefore, choose life and you and your descendants may live ..." (Deut. 30:19).

Reprinted from the *Catholic Mind* (December, 1968).